THE LIFE AND THOUGHT OF ST. EDITH STEIN

Visit our web site at
WWW.ALBAHOUSE.ORG

The Life and Thought of
ST. EDITH STEIN

Freda Mary Oben, PhD

A L B A · H O U S E   alba house   N E W · Y O R K

SOCIETY OF ST. PAUL, 2187 VICTORY BLVD., STATEN ISLAND, NEW YORK 10314

ST PAULS

Library of Congress Cataloging-in-Publication Data

Oben, Freda Mary.
    The life and thought of St. Edith Stein / Freda Mary Oben.
        p. cm.
    Includes bibliographical references (p.)
    ISBN 0-8189-0846-7
    1. Stein, Edith, Saint, 1891-1942. 2. Christian women saints—Germany—Biography. 3.
Discalced Carmelite nuns—Germany—Biography. 4. Christian converts from Judaism—
Germany—Biography. I. Title: Life and thought of Saint Edith Stein. II. Title.

BX4700.S74 O24 2000
282'.092 — dc21
[B]   00-044179

Produced and designed in the United States of America by the
Fathers and Brothers of the Society of St. Paul,
2187 Victory Boulevard, Staten Island, New York 10314-6603,
as part of their communications apostolate.

ISBN: 0-8189-0846-7

Printing Information:

Current Printing - first digit   1   2   3   4   5   6   7   8   9   10

Year of Current Printing - first year shown

2001   2002   2003   2004   2005   2006   2007   2008   2009   2010

In Loving Memory of My Jewish Family

Table of Contents

Biblical Abbreviations

OLD TESTAMENT

Genesis	Gn	Nehemiah	Ne	Baruch	Ba
Exodus	Ex	Tobit	Tb	Ezekiel	Ezk
Leviticus	Lv	Judith	Jdt	Daniel	Dn
Numbers	Nb	Esther	Est	Hosea	Ho
Deuteronomy	Dt	1 Maccabees	1 M	Joel	Jl
Joshua	Jos	2 Maccabees	2 M	Amos	Am
Judges	Jg	Job	Jb	Obadiah	Ob
Ruth	Rt	Psalms	Ps	Jonah	Jon
1 Samuel	1 S	Proverbs	Pr	Micah	Mi
2 Samuel	2 S	Ecclesiastes	Ec	Nahum	Na
1 Kings	1 K	Song of Songs	Sg	Habakkuk	Hab
2 Kings	2 K	Wisdom	Ws	Zephaniah	Zp
1 Chronicles	1 Ch	Sirach	Si	Haggai	Hg
2 Chronicles	2 Ch	Isaiah	Is	Malachi	Ml
Ezra	Ezr	Jeremiah	Jr	Zechariah	Zc
		Lamentations	Lm		

NEW TESTAMENT

Matthew	Mt	Ephesians	Eph	Hebrews	Heb
Mark	Mk	Philippians	Ph	James	Jm
Luke	Lk	Colossians	Col	1 Peter	1 P
John	Jn	1 Thessalonians	1 Th	2 Peter	2 P
Acts	Ac	2 Thessalonians	2 Th	1 John	1 Jn
Romans	Rm	1 Timothy	1 Tm	2 John	2 Jn
1 Corinthians	1 Cor	2 Timothy	2 Tm	3 John	3 Jn
2 Corinthians	2 Cor	Titus	Tt	Jude	Jude
Galatians	Gal	Philemon	Phm	Revelation	Rv

PART ONE

A Holy Life

CHAPTER 1

The Jewishness of Edith Stein

What *is* a life in face of so many of God's creatures? We can perhaps agree that a life well spent is a great deal, and that Edith Stein's was such a life.

How is a life well spent? Perhaps we look to the intentions of the actual person, to the contribution made to society, and, most of all, to the fulfillment of God's will in that life.

What were Edith's intentions? As child and adult, she wanted to love family and friends, she wanted to love the whole human race — which she did. As a German during World War I, she wanted to serve and to heal — which she did as a Red Cross nurse. As a female, she wanted to fight for women's rights — which she did, from a very young suffragette to the intellectual leader of the Catholic Women's Movement in Europe. Her hunger was to learn, understand truth, and philosophize — which she did as both philosopher and theologian; and despite her humility, her seminal work which wedded phenomenology to scholasticism is very important. As a Catholic, she wanted to be holy — and she was, both as secular woman and contemplative nun. She wanted her entire life to be formed by love of God — and it was.

As a convert, she wanted to be faithful to her Jewish heritage, to share the fate of the Jews during the Holocaust in imitation of Christ's passion, and to expiate for the human sins causing the evil of the Shoah. And she did — to the point of martyrdom!

These were her contributions to society. As to God's will in her life, Edith had a steadfast faith in God's providence; in fact, she believed that God had worked out a specific plan for her life unto the last detail. She trusted and surrendered to that divine will.

Cannot we say that she chose wisely? And when she finally stepped through the door of that little white cottage where she died at Auschwitz, despite the physical agony of the gas, let us dare to say that, in a piercing recognition of martyrdom, her joy was great because she had become "another Christ."

We have said Edith believed in God's plan for her. Surely, it is no accident that Edith Stein was born a Jewess and became a Catholic: she is the fruit of both faiths. That is the unique essence of her holiness. She is a symbol of that new person born through Christ's reconciliation of Jew and gentile on the cross, described by St. Paul (Eph 2:14-16). As a sign of the sacred link between both faiths, she deepens our understanding and respect for each other.

Let us therefore see her in the first part of her life as a Jewess, the first thirty of her fifty lived years. We will depict her in a family community of love, of an inherited social consciousness which conceives the whole of humanity as God's family and one's personal responsibility as a member of that family. She witnessed Jewish religiosity, prayer, and the need for expiation, and we recognize these traits in Edith.

We can understand Edith's later desire to share in Christ's redemptive action as a flowering of the Judaic seeds within her. In olden days on "Yom Kippur," the day of Atonement (which actually fell on her day of birth, October 12, 1891), on this day her forefathers once sacrificed a kid, ram or lamb. Even today, the rabbi still prays, "From this day shall be made an atonement for you to cleanse you that you may be clean from all your sins before the Lord" (*The Form,* 327-28). At the end of the 24-hour fast, the "Shofar" is blown which announces a new birth into freedom from sin. The impact which all this made on Edith is obvious in her later life. She also tells us that this was her favorite holiday as a youngster; she could stay late in bed and read before she had to dress for appearance at the synagogue!

Let us imagine little "Jitschel" (this was Edith's nickname, a Polish idiom meaning child), as a pretty four-year-old running merrily about with her friends between the piles of logs in her mother's lumberyard. Or perhaps we can picture the four-year-old prodigy on the shoulder of her eldest brother Paul as she happily repeats his quotations from Goethe and Schiller. Again, there is a very disappointed four-year-old who, dressed in her best, has waited vainly for the family of her little friend to pick her up for an outing on the Promenade. Next day she declares to the little culprit, "Whoever lies once is never believed, even when he speaks the truth!" (Even then, how important truth was to her.) We can assume the little culprit suffered miserably for what she considered an injustice: she had expected Edith to come to them rather than be picked up; yet this child was to become one of Edith's goddaughters.

Edith had indeed been a willful child, like many of our saints. But at the age of seven, she experienced a minor conversion: she suddenly realized, when watching a person in a fit of anger, how ugly it was for her to throw a tantrum. She becomes quiet and obedient. She describes how cognizant she was now of the people and happenings about her and that she ponders over them. She writes that this was the beginning for her of a secret, inner life. Could this be the beginning of her potential as a contemplative? Throughout her life, people knew of her reserve.

Her avidity for knowledge sprang to the fore early. How

could a four-year-old who could recite Goethe and Schiller be content with attending kindergarten? She refused and was finally allowed to enter first grade in 1897 on her sixth birthday. But this was mid-semester, before the school would normally have admitted her. This was the Breslau Victoriaschule, formerly the Old Schaffgott Palace on the Ritterplatz.

She was, of course, a brilliant student, made much of at home as well as at school. Her home — what a wonderful portrait of family life Edith has drawn for us in the autobiography of her youth, *Life in a Jewish Family*. In fact, it is a veritable gallery of family portraits, starting with her late 18th century ancestors. What an assemblage of figures she presents, depicting a community of spirituality through the generations, one of sacrifice and love which certainly influenced our saint. Indeed, the members of her immediate family stay constantly with Edith in her journey and travail for they form a great part of her motivation in a personal self-offering.

Let us first speak of Edith's maternal line. She has given us much more information here, beginning with her great-grandfather, Joseph Burchard, born in 1785. His marriage to Ernestine Praeger rendered eleven children. Their home in Silesia contained a special room, where he prayed with his sons and sons-in-law and taught liturgy to his grandsons. His position as Cantor in the synagogue gave way later to the manufacturing of surgical cotton in his own factory.

Edith's beautiful comments about her revered great-grandparents make note of the fact that, in their old age, their needs were provided for by their children. But even though by that time they were poor, her great-grandparents managed to spare food and clothing for others. Ernestine taught her grandchildren as she had her children to sew for the poor, and one of these little ones was Augusta, Edith's mother, who also read to her grandmother and remembered her as a truly pious woman.

Ernestine outlived her husband by many years, finally living with her daughter Adelheid who had married Salomon Courant: these two are described vividly by their granddaughter Edith. Ernestine also outlived this daughter who had worked very hard all her life. As a mere child, Adelheid had risen early to sew, for her father did not earn enough as Cantor. One sees readily the example made by Adelheid on Augusta, one of fifteen children: she saw her mother work hard as bookkeeper in the family business, despite her 15 children. Augusta was trained by her mother from the age of four, along with the other children, to help in the house and the grocery store.

The family did not study the Talmud daily, but on Saturdays they prayed and held discussions. As Augusta did later in her own home, the Courant family followed the Jewish prescriptions, although they were not strictly orthodox. Salomon actually started a Jewish school for his own sons and those of the neighbors. The sons were formally educated and became professionals, but, of course, this was not so for the girls. Very important, again an attitude followed by Augusta, they were taught to respect other religions.

Portraits of the grandparents Adelheid and Salomon hung on the wall over the sofa in Augusta's living room. Adelheid's picture shows suffering and sadness. Edith was told of the wisdom and charisma of her grandmother, who died before Edith was born. Not only did Augusta and the other children come to Adelheid for advice, but many women of nobility from the surrounding area likewise did so.

On the other hand, the picture of Salomon is entirely jovial. Edith remembers his jokes and the chocolates which he gave to all the children, apparently even to strangers. The grocery store had prospered and he, too, remembered to give to the poor. Edith describes visiting him in his large house in Lublinitz as a toddler. It was on the occasion of his 80th birthday, and this big family party was Edith's first. Her grandfather died three years later when she was five.

Let us talk of Edith's mother, Augusta. What a wonderful woman! Interestingly, she attended a Catholic elementary school from the age of 5 to 12. At eight, she could run the house for Adelheid and help in the store. Gustel, that was her nickname, sewed and read at the same time all her life. Her brothers were sent to the gymnasium, but she was taken out of school at age 12. This may well have encouraged her readiness for the advanced education of Edith and her other daughters. Augusta did receive further instructions in German and French, and she could play the piano. She and her sisters learned Hebrew from the Jewish teachers who came to the elementary school, but they never attained a fluency or even an understanding of the language. Also, they learned the prescriptions in German, not Hebrew, a practice which Augusta continued with her own children.

Now we come to Edith's paternal side. Augusta met her future husband, Siegfried Stein, when she was 9 years old; he was 15. They married when she was 21, he 27. Siegfried's grandfather Joseph — that is, Edith's great-grandfather — had been born in 1776. He was a merchant and a respected Prussian citizen. His death at the age of 36 in 1812 was officially recorded. He had three sons, one of whom was Simon, Siegfried's father, born the very year his father died.

Simon had three marriages which produced 23 children! His last wife was Johanna Cohn, the mother of Siegfried. This enterprising lady conducted a lumberyard in Gleiwitz, after her husband's death, called "S. Stein's Widow." Here Siegfried brought his bride Augusta, and here they had five children and lost one.

They then moved to Augusta's hometown of Lublinitz, hoping her parents would help them start their own lumberyard. This did not materialize well; instead, Augusta lived through the death of her mother Adelheid. In Easter, 1890, they moved to Breslau with two more children, three having died in infancy. They lived on Köhlenstrasse where Edith was born (this street no longer exists). We can imagine that after the death of four babies, Edith, their last child, must indeed have been precious to the Steins.

Edith writes that she was fascinated by Augusta's total absorption in God and felt she was doubly precious to her mother for having been born on the "Yom Kippur" of that year; Augusta took it as a special sign of God's blessing on the life of her child. As we have said, Edith loved this feast above all the other holidays. Their business was conducted on Saturdays; yet the Stein household was conscious of its Jewish heritage and faithful to it.

For Edith, her mother ever remained the ideal of the proverbial woman found in Hebrew Scripture, strong in love, courage and industry. Mrs. Stein, after her husband's death at the age of 48, actually ran the lumberyard, and, at the age of 84, she was still occupied helping out in the office. Edith always writes lovingly of her mother. This love is not only a great part of her own spirituality but is the core of her future ontology of the woman. Augusta is a model of spiritual maternity. Although her mother conducted the business, and the elder daughters Elsa and Frieda helped care for the smaller children, she still remained the heart of the home.

They kept a kosher home although many of their close friends did not. The home was a fine one, built at the end of the 18th or beginning of the 19th century. They were helped by maids. Their address was now 38 Michaelistrasse, where they had moved when Edith was in high school. It was a huge house, architecturally quite beautifully made, a large brick building covered with grey plaster. (This house is now in Polish territory, in the city of Wroclaw, on "Nowowiepka" Street.) There is a nearby park, still a favorite place where children play, a pond where they can skate and slide in winter on the ice. It is easy to picture the nature lover Edith enjoying it also at that time.

Edith writes that her mother had 12 siblings, the names of whom the children were required to memorize and recite like the 12 tribes of Israel. Mrs. Stein was proud of being Jewish and she taught the children to respect their faith. Yet, let us remember that she also taught them to respect other faiths. Many of their friends were Christians, and when they reached adulthood, some of them seemed to be assimilated, no longer following the traditional prescriptions. We will see later that part of Augusta's agony concerning Edith's conversion was that she wondered if she were not herself partly responsible for not having raised Edith more strictly in the Jewish faith.

Edith remembers the wonderful Jewish characteristics of generosity and love, of family closeness. Just as her great-grandmother and grandmother had given to the poor, so did Augusta give cash as well as free wood to her impoverished customers. And just as Augusta at the age of 8 had been sent out of town to nurse a sick relative and had cared for her own sister Mikha after a stroke, so did Edith volunteer to help her aunt when the 75-year-old was left alone.

These close family ties continued when the children reached adulthood. Augusta ran the business with the help of Arno, and he took over when she could no longer take charge. Erna lived with Augusta after her marriage to Hans Biberstein and even conducted her medical practice in the house for a while; in fact, her two children Susan and Harold were born there. Paul tried the lumberyard for a while, but it was not right for him so he worked in a bank. Rosa took care of the house. Elsa taught before she married Max Gordon and moved to Hamburg. Frieda's arranged marriage had failed; she returned to live at home, and her baby, Erika Tworoger, looked at picture books on the floor as Aunt Edith studied. Eventually Frieda worked as bookkeeper in the family business.

We can say that Edith had very happy memories of her entire youth. She was given an example of compassion and service, of an ecumenical outlook, of hard work, and great respect for education.

Edith's formation as a person makes an organic whole: she lived what she wrote and she wrote what she lived. After all, what we each want is to augment our own personhood, to totally fulfill its potential in the eyes of God. And this was Edith's overriding purpose in her works.

We have seen that her own genius as a child was recognized and fostered, yet in early puberty, a blight hit her soul. She deliberately and consciously stopped praying, and soon announced that she wanted to drop out of school! This was in 1906 when she was fourteen and a half years old, in the 9th grade. A mixup in the school structure would have necessitated her losing a year, but, already in the seventh grade, she had started not being up to par. Her mother very wisely sent her to help her married sister Elsa in Hamburg who actually needed moral support at the time.

Although Edith dropped out of school, she still continued to read avidly; some of the works she chose were by the Austrian playwright Grillparzer as well as by the German poet and playwright Hebbel, Ibsen, Shakespeare, Schopenhauer! When she was almost 16, she decided to go back to school. She had to make up three years and she did it in six months with the help of private tutoring in Latin and Mathematics; on her own she reviewed French, English and History. Her exams were in Easter of 1908 and she was then able to enter high-school, termed there *Obersecunda*.

As a high-school student, Edith was in the thick of it: friends, fun and activities. She had many friends, although her sister Erna Biberstein assured me once that Edith never had a real boyfriend. But in an intimate circle, she played tennis, rowed, danced, and took part in winter sports including skiing. She was proud of her virginity, yet flirted with her cousins! She was director and prompter of her class play at graduation.

The child who had so loved vacationing with her family in the country continued to revel in nature, hiking and picnicking. She would stretch out on a deer look-out. In order to lie on the grass, she would coil her hair over her ears "like snail shells." There, watching the sky, mountains, and woods, she was apt to be reading Spinoza. Certainly, Edith must have experienced much joy in order to analyze such difficult material so well in her writings. One of her youthful friends remembers Edith as "very gay, and with a marvelous sense of humor; she had a dimple on her chin which they all loved, and when she laughed, her beautiful grey eyes shone" (Stein, *Aus der Tiefe*, 14). Her friends even then thought her empathetic: for despite her modesty and inner reserve, she was a very caring person, listening and helping them when needed.

She loved children, and her nephews and nieces adored and respected her. She was detached and yet friendly, asking about their own interests and schoolwork, writing skits and poems for their parties. Little nephew Helmut proposed to Edith at Erna's engagement party, and they celebrated their union by Helmut sitting on Edith's lap and eating her portion of cake! The children always remained dear to her, and she maintained contact with them even from the convent.

In 1911 she entered the University of Breslau, among the early group of women to be matriculated there. Here she studied for two years in psychology, philosophy, history and German philology. It is rather amusing that, at this time, this self-declared "atheist" found psychology wanting, asserting that it had no soul! There is another amusing tale that she tells on herself. One of her friends said to her, "You seem to have become far too critical." And she confesses, "I had been living in the naive conviction that I was perfect.... I had always considered it my privilege to make remarks about everything I found negative, inexorably pointing out other persons' weaknesses, mistakes, or faults of which I became aware, often using a ridiculing or sarcastic tone of voice. There were persons who found me 'enchantingly malicious'" (Stein, *Life*, 195-96). This lady was later to say that nothing is gained by telling people off.

So, this high-spirited girl loved people, the arts, nature, the theater, music, painting (she could draw, too), but she could also be extremely keen in philosophical discourse. And Edith in her reserve can already be viewed as a solitary journeyer despite her great empathy and sociability. It is no wonder that she was to consider the formation of personhood as the kernel of human existence.

Later she was to say that the one who is seeking the truth is really seeking for God, whether he knows it or not. At that time, she did not know this. In her college days, her personal traits of love and empathy enabled her to go only part-way on the journey: i.e., she related to her fellow creatures in charity. In 1912, she read a novel depicting young people in the grip of amorality due to alcoholism; this threw her into sadness, so deep was her relatedness and caring for others. That evening she went to a concert where they played Martin Luther's hymn, "A Mighty Fortress is Our God." But she is not yet thinking of God as the answer. Instead, she decides that, as long as she and her friends stand together, they will overcome any evil. At that time, humanity was her solution to human problems. But soon, of course, her answer becomes the Passion of Christ.

Already as a high-school student, she had campaigned as an ardent suffragette. She eagerly read the daily newspaper and loved to discuss current events. Now she declared in discussions with her college friends that she would never give up a career for marriage. And yet she tells us in her autobiography that she had always dreamed of a happy married life.

But now, in 1913, she was preparing to leave the University of Breslau for the University of Göttingen to study under Edmund Husserl, the famous founder of the school of phenomenology. She had read his text, *Logical Investigations*, and in it found everything that was lacking in the field of psychology. Her friends teased her with a rhyme: "Whereas other young ladies dreamed of *Busserl* [kisses], Edith dreams only of Husserl!" (Posselt, 20).

Edith was immediately attracted to the objectivity and realism of Husserl's philosophical approach. It seemed indeed to be the purest of sciences as it analyzed and described the essence of all phenomena, of all human experience that seems to be given to consciousness. Phenomenology asks, "What can we really know" and "How is it that we really can know it?"

This philosophical group was largely composed of Jews. A friend of Edith, Hedwig Conrad-Martius, who was a philosopher and member of the group, writes of the affinity between what she calls the Jewish radical spirit and phenomenology. A movement of conversion sprang up amidst these great thinkers. Husserl was himself a convert from Judaism to the Lutheran Church. There was now a spirituality which we can recognize as part of the Religious Revival taking place in Europe and America.

For the last three centuries, Christian ontological principles had remained unrecognized by philosophy. Now Husserl's insistence on the reality of the objective world included the reality of the supernatural. Divine Being was no longer considered a subjective concern. Instead, Peter Wust writes that we have "a searching back for objectivity to the sacredness of being, to the purity and chasteness of things, 'of the thing in itself'" (Oben, *Edith Stein*, 12).

The young students of Göttingen were more influenced

by Max Scheler, also a Jewish convert, than they were by Husserl. And Edith writes that Scheler's lectures laid the basis for her Catholicism. "The barriers of rationalistic prejudice with which I had unwittingly grown up fell and the world of faith unfolded before me" (*Life*, 260). Scheler lectured on religious subjects such as humility and sanctity. Stein tells us that she knew now she had to investigate what seemed to be reality to these very brilliant minds. To the searcher of truth, this meant reality wherever it led.

She made friends with another Jewish professor and his wife, Adolf and Anna Reinach. She found a kind of personal goodness here different from what she had always taken for granted from her family. Edith describes the Philosophical Circle to which she belonged, the heady discussions that went on, herself, of course, being quite audible. One of the members, Hans Lipps, was especially interesting to her, but the promise of a romantic tie never materialized.

During these happy years at Göttingen, Edith would take little trips with friends and family: when she visited the former homes of Goethe and Schiller in Weimar, she must have remembered the four-year-old on the back of Paul who recited poetry. Then World War I broke out and everything changed. The men started to go to the front; Adolf Reinach was among the very first. Edith was very patriotic; in fact, she was a passionate Prussian! Roman Ingarden writes, "...she went through the entire war with the attitude of someone always on the verge of beginning a one-man battle... she wrote me letter after letter asking whether she had the right to waste her time on philosophy and other such nonsense when there were people out there dying whom she should be helping" (Herbstrith, *Edith Stein* [Harper, 1985], 82).

She went to help the wounded and dying as a Red Cross Nurse, stopping her studies in April of 1915. This brave woman actually applied to serve at the front. But she was assigned to nurse the soldiers infected with spotted fever, dysentery, and cholera at the Epidemic Hospital in Weisskirchen, Austria. Her own account of this period is extremely revealing of her as a person. It shows her great generosity and courage, of course (these were all contagious diseases); but it also shows a practical side of her nature which enabled her to face many sensitive and difficult situations.

"Sister Edith," as she was called, was tireless, caring ardently about each patient. Those who could not eat on their own she spoon-fed a mixture of egg made with cognac and red wine, and diluted with sugar water! Those unable to bathe themselves she bathed or sponged as if they were small children. She would anoint a man who was covered with scabies from hand to foot.

Sometimes she was filled with despair at her inability to help a patient live. After work, she would have strong coffee and cigarettes to calm her nerves. Small wonder that worry about her patients kept her from sleeping at night! When the typhoid cases lessened, she willingly went to the surgical room, to help bandage the patients. With her she had brought her doctoral manuscript, a copy of Homer and of Husserl's *Ideen.* Her keen intellect was useful now as she memorized the questions and answers given in nine languages in a small manual, so that she could better communicate with the patients who came from all parts of the Austrian-Hungarian Empire!

Edith had known before she came that the Lazaretto was morally lax, which did not frighten her. She maintained very cordial relations with the staff but did not attend the parties. There is a very funny incident when one of the doctors tried to hold her hand during a medical procedure. She withdrew it, saying nothing. But the next morning she marched into his office and gave him a very hard time. The poor fellow was afraid to even look her way again.

In September, she went home on furlough and then volunteered to do further work for the Red Cross, but was not called back. She had served six months. She returned to Göttingen and, in 1916, was awarded the doctorate *summa cum laude*. Mrs. Husserl and her daughter Elli made her a crown of ivy and daisies, announcing that in Edith's "glow of happiness," she looked "just like a Queen" (*Life*, 412). Little did this queen know that, in not too many years, she would wear the crown of martyrdom.

It is no wonder that, given Edith's own natural gift of empathy and interest in interpersonal relationships, that her doctoral thesis was *On the Problem of Empathy*. This work was so good that it was soon published in 1917. The men of the philosophical circle at Göttingen were away at war. Edith was the most brilliant woman there, and it is a wonderful testimony of her genius that Husserl asked her to be his first assistant at the University of Freiburg to which he was now transferring.

Unfortunately, Edith was very disappointed in her post there. She did enjoy teaching Husserl's beginning students, to whom she referred as her "philosophical kindergarten." She transcribed and edited his notes for publication, but she was not given enough scope to exercise her independence and originality. She writes early in 1918 to her friend Roman Ingarden: "And if Husserl will not accustom himself once more to treat me as a collaborator in the work — as I have always considered our situation to be and he, in theory, did likewise — then we shall have to part company" (Stein, *Self-Portrait*, 22).

Even the great beauty of the nearby Black Forest could not compensate for her frustration. She stayed only eighteen months. But while she was there, she had managed to write fine studies which were soon published in 1922 and gave her a name in the discipline: *Psychische Kausalität (Psychic Causality)* and *Individuum und Gemeinschaft (The Individual and the Community)*, both as yet unpublished in English translation. After leaving Husserl, she campaigned for the German Democratic Party. This augmented her interest in human relationships and human rights; the result was her work *Untersuchung über den Staat* (*The State*), published in 1925, not yet translated into English. We will examine these works in our treatment of her philosophy of the person.

Something had happened in 1917. Adolf had died at the front, and she had come to help Anna arrange his papers. This was the great turning point in Edith's life. She expected that she would have to console the widow, but, instead, she found a strong person who consoled her. Anna and Adolf had both become Lutherans before he died. Edith testified much later to a priest that she recognized in Anna (in this we recognize Edith's empathy) a deep kinship with the crucified Christ. From then on, Edith said, Judaism paled and the cross loomed high before her.

It took her five years to make a decisive step, and these were difficult years. She had hoped to attain a university post where she could do her *habilitation*, which is another doctoral thesis written while teaching on a university level. This never materialized: she was a Jewess and a woman, hardly the usual type of professor. She taught privately in Breslau and wrote works which revealed a more spiritual bent. Already in writing *Psychic Causality*, she had acquired enough insight to describe the center of a person's inner being where a receptivity enables one to rest in God; surrender to God here yields a burst of renewed life (Stein, *Psychische Kausalität*, 76).

An incident took place one day when she entered the Catholic Cathedral in Frankfurt and saw a woman stop for private prayer. This was a new experience for Edith: before then, she had witnessed only public liturgy, but this seemed such a personal matter between the woman and God. There is a beautiful Catholic church in Breslau near Edith's home, St. Michael's. We know she attended Mass there after her baptism; perhaps, she went before.

She writes later that faith is a seizure by God, and that presupposes becoming seized. The person turned away from God can refuse to turn to Him even if touched by Him. The convert is the one who, in hearing God's call, turns to Him in perfect, free acceptance. We cannot believe without grace, but even grace depends on the person's free assent and cooperation.

A Jewish friend testifies that Edith, in her search for truth, was trying in fairness at that time to read the Hebrew Scriptures. We know that her love for the psalms stayed with her throughout her life: in fact, her translation of Psalm 61 (60 in English collections) was included in the German book of Common Prayer. How fitting for her are the psalmist's words of yearning for God. "Take pity on me, God, take pity on me / In you my soul takes shelter / I take shelter in the shadow of your wings / until the destroying storm is over." In one of her high school courses in German Literature she was introduced to the New Testament, and we can believe that she was reading it at this point in her life.

Edith was physically affected by her spiritual crisis; at the time of her sister Erna's wedding in 1920, she suffered painful stomach cramps. She was holding her great secret within her, speaking of it to no one, except to God. The wedding took place in their home, and Edith prepared the large parlor for the ceremony. She writes that, before the actual ceremony, "At a Jewish wedding, the bride waits seated in a place set apart.... We put Erna's seat against a column between two windows where my desk usually stood. Above it hung a painting of St. Francis by Cimabue.... I looked at St. Francis above her head and found great consolation in his presence" (*Life*, 238).

Ever the scientist, Edith was also searching objectively for ultimate reality, God. Now she knew she wanted to be a Christian, but did not know which way to go: Scheler had prepared her for Catholicism, but many of her friends were Protestant.

Of course, we know now that it was the reading of Teresa of Avila's autobiography one summer night in 1921 which brought her into the Catholic Church.

She was visiting her friends, Hans and Hedwig Conrad-Martius. This was actually a fruit farm where the former members of the Philosophy Circle would come to help gather the fruit and enjoy their philosophical talks. Hedwig describes Edith as being particularly reserved and quiet at that time. One evening, Edith was left to entertain herself with a book. We can be certain it was not by accident that she picked up the *Life* of Teresa.

What happened that wonderful night? The psalmist sings: "My heart is ready, God, my heart is ready" (Psalm 57). She is taught by Teresa, whom she calls a master psychologist. Teresa writes that it is not science and knowledge that is needed in faith, rather it is humility and surrender to God. But, most important, Teresa discloses her own personal experience of the Person of Christ.

In a later work, Edith writes that no one can call Christ "Lord" unless He is revealed by the Holy Spirit: and it is the same Spirit that spoke through the prophets! Edith is truly seized by divine fire and supernatural love. Truth is present to her now in the Person of Christ, a truth she had been seeking through various phases during the last decade. She had actually read through the entire night; at dawn, she closed the book and said, "That is the truth" (Posselt, 64). Along with Zechariah, she could rejoice: "In the tender compassion of our God / the dawn from on high shall break upon us, / to shine on those who dwell in darkness and the shadow of death, / and to guide our feet into the way of peace."

Christ is henceforth to be the paradigm not only for her, but for everyone, in her philosophy of the person. Absolute Truth for her, His way becomes her life. She writes later that it is not a system of philosophy that is needed by the person but a way of life. For her, a simple living faith is closer to divine wisdom than all philosophical and theological science. It is to bring persons to the faith that she will become a Christian philosopher.

Edith is now an integrated personality because her intellectual and spiritual formation are fused into one. This integration is the core of her creativity as philosopher-theologian. So authentic is her teaching that, through her scholarship and prayer, she becomes God's mouthpiece.

She is also to be His instrument. After her baptism, Edith reveled in her blood-tie to Christ. We will see the connection between her family ties and her life offering. She was now to follow perfectly the Jewish injunctions: "And thou shalt love the Lord thy God, with all thy heart, and with all thy soul, and with all thy might" (Dt 6:5) and "thou shalt love thy neighbor as thyself: I am the Lord" (Lv 19:18). As we continue, we will understand that Christ Himself gives witness to His love, in her.

CHAPTER 2

The New Convert: Phenomenology and Thomas Aquinas

L et us visualize our God-filled young lady at the dawn of a summer morning in 1921. She was 29, but for her it was the dawn of a whole new life, as a Catholic. She had just closed the book of *The Life of St. Teresa of Avila* and had said, "That is the truth." Being the self-reliant, methodical person that Edith Stein was, she went directly to buy a Catechism and a Missal to prepare for baptism. When she felt herself ready, she went to the local parish priest in Bergzabern, Father Breitling of St. Martin's Church, and asked him to baptize her.

One can easily say that he was surprised, and even more astounded when he saw, after a few questions, how ready she was! Nevertheless, he scheduled some meetings with her and finally set the following January 1st for her baptism.

At home in Breslau, Edith met with the Chaplain of Breslau University. He suggested that she read Thomas Aquinas during her period of waiting. Surely this was no accident. Pius X had recently written, "If the Church has ever approved or promoted the doctrine of any author or Saint, this is only insofar as that doctrine adheres to the principles of Aquinas and is in no way opposed to them."

At this time, then, there was real fervor for the teachings of Aquinas. In 1879, Pope Leo XIII had issued the encyclical *Aeterni Patris* ("On the Restoration of Christian Philosophy According to the Mind of St. Thomas Aquinas, the Angelic Doctor").

The letter was directed against the irreligious humanism of that day. He writes, "Evil teaching about things, human and divine, has come forth from the schools of philosophers" (*Aeterni Patris*, vii). But if philosophy is used well, it supports and defends faith.

He argued that the First Fathers had understood Christ as the "wisdom of God." Their doctrines were studied by the doctors of the Middle Ages, the Scholastics, who tried to tie together human and divine knowledge. The greatest Scholastic of them all was Thomas Aquinas, whom he recommends to all students of philosophy. Not only will philosophy itself be healed on such a secure footing, but all errors in human science will be refuted, as well as in civil society and family life.

Edith writes that in herself "St. Thomas found a reverent and willing disciple." What an exciting encounter this must have been! Of course, she had known something of Aquinas through Husserl who had said that phenomenology "converges towards Thomism and prolongs Thomism" (Mirabel, 73). But from then on, Thomas was to be an important mentor leading her in intellectual and spiritual growth.

She studied him gladly in order to learn the intellectual foundations of the faith. And we may be sure that her keen mind, trained in phenomenology, immediately made comparisons between Husserl and Aquinas. How amazing that the crossroad in her life, her conversion, now afforded her the unique ability to recognize an interconnection of the two disciplines: phenomenology and Thomism. Actually, it was necessary for *her* to understand any and all possible bridges between them. We will see that this keen interest not only bestowed goodness on both disciplines: it provided her a path to follow as a Christian philosopher.

In St. Thomas she found the balance of learning, wisdom and faith which creates harmony leading to truth. Before, the phenomenological method had enabled her to find kernels of truth in the discovery of pure essence. Now, through the philosopher-theologian Aquinas, she recognizes that it is through the way of faith that wisdom is found, not through scientific analysis. For perfect philosophical thought is accessible through both "reason and revelation in an all inclusive unity" (*Endliches und Ewiges Sein*, 27). She will be a Christian philosopher preparing the way for faith.

Her happiness at this point must have been unbounded. She prepared in a night vigil for her baptism on New Year's Day of 1922, choosing the baptismal name of Teresa. On that day when she was brought into the Church, she also received Holy Communion which would become a daily practice. She wanted to become a Religious immediately, and, of course, wanted to go into Carmel where St. Teresa had been, but that was not to be. Her spiritual director counseled her to wait: she was too important as a laywoman and, for her mother, the attending pain would be unbearable.

Now, what of her mother? Edith's sister Erna told me that Edith asked her to tell Augusta about the baptism. Erna answered, "Tell her yourself." Edith told her mother, and for the first time in her life, Edith saw her mother break down and weep profusely. They cried together. The terrible thing is that, for the Steins, the word Catholic held only menial connotations, such as of maids they had had whom they imagined would grovel on their knees and kiss the priest's toe! But a family friend does testify that Mrs. Stein recognized in some way, because she was religious herself, that grace had taken over the entire being of her daughter. She radiated holiness. They saw that Edith had become another person. As Teresa of Avila writes, "In one moment God was pleased to make me another person." And so it was with Edith Stein.

We wonder, did this lover of the psalms perhaps think of Psalm 23 as did the Fathers of the Church in relation to baptism? They describe it as a celebration of its mystery.

> The Lord is my shepherd; I shall not want.
> In verdant pastures he gives me repose;
> Beside restful waters he leads me;
> He refreshes my soul.
> He guides me in right paths for his name's sake.
> Even though I walk in the dark valley
> I fear no evil; for you are at my side
> With your rod and your staff
> that give me courage.

Christ is the shepherd who initiates souls in His mysteries, bringing them to the waters of refreshment where the soul "is bedewed with divine gifts to produce good fruits." The soul is led to green pastures, "the Church of God in which His saints flower." The real conversion of the soul is the introduction to the path of justice (Quasten, 325-332).

Her spiritual director was Canon Schwind of the Cathedral in Speyer. At his suggestion she went to teach there for the Dominican nuns at their Teachers' College and girls' academy, St. Magdalena. She took private vows of chastity, poverty and obedience and led a very intense life of prayer and work. And there was always a great deal of work. She taught the young girls, nuns, and novices and from this developed her deep interest in the essence, the psyche, of the woman.

Her interest in Aquinas produced seminal works. She wanted to know what was in his text *Quaestiones disputatae de veritate* (*Truth*), and so she translated it from the Latin at the suggestion of Father Erich Przywara who became her good friend and mentor. This was not only a translation — it was accompanied by a commentary from the phenomenological point of view. This was something new, and it brought her a great deal of acclaim. She also translated the letters of Cardinal Newman from English into German. She started what she hoped would be her habilitation, calling it "Potenz und Akt" (Act and Potency), a takeoff from Aquinas. But most important was a comparative study, "Husserls Phänomenologie und die Philosophie des hl. Thomas von Aquino" (*Husserl's Phenomenology and the Philosophy of St. Thomas Aquinas*). In her first version, she actually sets the two in a dialogue as they discuss their philosophies. This was a very important step in a new direction.

This comparative study of 1929 was so important that, three years later, when a Thomistic conference was held in France on just that very question, she was the only woman invited to attend the session. She was not asked to speak (being a woman, perhaps?), but the records of the day show that she dominated the discussion. The important Thomistic scholars there were absolutely delighted with her renditions in French and German — Berdiaev, Gilson, Maritain, Koyré, etc. (See *"La Phénoménologie"*; also Posselt, 46).

But just what is phenomenology and how does it compare to Thomism? This is a very interesting and important question.

Although the term phenomenology was used before Husserl, he is considered the founder of this branch of philosophy at the turn of the 20th century. It seeks to analyze and describe the world as we experience it, persons, events, objects, concepts. We ask, how can we know things outside of ourselves, and how does this knowledge become our own? The phenomenologist believes: that which reveals itself as itself takes place in consciousness. So, only that which is absolutely given to consciousness is absolutely known.

Now there is a difference between the natural attitude in

which we view things and the world, and the phenomenological attitude which reflects upon this natural attitude. All preconceived theories are "bracketed off" as it were. The only certitude is one's personal, original experience of the phenomenon.

How is this done? Here we use a basic term in phenomenology: "intentionality." This does not mean "I do this in order to do that." It means that my consciousness is relating to something: it is conscious of or experiencing something that I see, imagine, remember, or judge. Hence, phenomenology is called "a descriptive philosophy of experience."

It is the *essence* of the thing which the phenomenologist seeks, and this is achieved through a process called "eidetic intuition." This puts into play a free, imaginative plan, when we remove certain characteristics from the object to be known. If some features are removed, the object will remain intact, while others if removed would destroy the object itself. Edith Stein writes, "To the essence of *this man*, it belongs that he easily flies into a rage, is easily appeased, that he loves music and likes to have people around him. It does not belong to his essence that he just now went into the street and was surprised by rain..." (Baseheart, *Person*, 55). This result of *reflection* is termed "phenomenological reduction" or "free variation."

Although Edith did not follow Husserl in the line of transcendental thought to which he later turned, she always remained his disciple and used his method through all her work. Yet she remains independent of Husserl. First, in her work on St. Thomas she turns to metaphysics, which was not Husserl's idea of a strict science. Also, she uses the work of other philosophers, whereas Husserl held phenomenology to be a science of new beginnings. This comparative study was published in a special *Festschrift* on the occasion of Husserl's 70th birthday, in the 1929 Yearbook for Philosophy and Phenomenological Research. (This work has been translated: see Stein, *Knowledge and Faith*).

The two philosophers, Husserl and Aquinas, are presented through five basic themes. Edith notes their differences and likenesses. First, Husserl and Aquinas both consider philosophy to be a strict, objective science based on reason and geared to attain a knowledge of being. But for Husserl, philosophy means phenomenology, while to Aquinas it means metaphysics.

Second, Husserl accepts natural reason as the way to truth, while for Aquinas it is reason enlightened by faith. We shall see that later, in *Endliches und ewiges Sein* (*Finite and Eternal Being*), her definitive work, Edith follows Aquinas in using revelation to help philosophy attain a "deeper and more comprehensive knowledge of being."

Third, on the question of Being, Stein acknowledges that Husserl's first principle is that of transcendental consciousness, while the first principle of Aquinas is God. What is fascinating to us is that, in *EES*, Edith will use as her starting point in the ascent to God an awareness of her own body. In doing so, she uses Husserl's immediate knowledge of the "pure I," the self known through consciousness, and also Aquinas' immediate knowledge of the soul.

The fourth theme of comparison is Essence and Existence. Here there is real common ground and is one reason why phenomenology was referred to as a revival of Scholasticism. Both philosophers distinguish between that which belongs to itself (its essence), and that which is accidental to it. Edith claims that Aquinas' distinction between essence and existence preceded Husserl's notion of bracketing. In Scholastic philosophy, contingent being (i.e., you or I) has its own essence but receives its existence. With self-evident Being, God, His essence *is* His existence.

Fifth, she asks if Husserl's concept of intuition is like that of Aquinas' abstraction of essence. Both agree that the knowledge of essence is based on the intellect's action on the material of the senses; Husserl himself noted the likeness of his "ideating" to abstraction where the universal is gathered from the particular. The "ratio" of Aquinas is the abstraction of a whole independent of accidental parts.

Also in the *Festschrift*, Edith discusses the question of the immediacy of knowledge. Both Husserl and Aquinas agree that it is the light of the intellect which provides knowledge of essences. Here, Stein writes, they agree on knowledge of the exterior world. But Husserl puts knowledge of God beyond the scope of phenomenology; with Aquinas, his intellectual light participates in God's light as he reveals knowledge of the interior world. His investigation of essences discloses data of both natural experience and faith.

Stein's procedure will come from both teachers. But because she uses the phenomenological language and method to present certain Thomistic concepts, she presents new insights, new meanings. But we will see that, ultimately, she arises independently from both.

One of the lectures which she gave during these years at Speyer dealt with the topic, "The Intellect and the Intellectuals," based on Aquinas. She gave many lectures on Aquinas, as well as on the woman, at conferences and over the radio. These were attended not only by women but by men; in fact, by priests. She became what has been termed "the intellectual leader" of the Catholic Women's Movement in Europe during the years 1928 to 1933, which ended, of course, when Hitler became Reich Chancellor of Germany.

She had wanted to become a religious, and when she came to Speyer this was the closest to the real thing. It was a Catholic atmosphere of prayer and seclusion. One can imagine that she took on this humble post as a gesture of total self-giving and great generosity of soul as thanks for her gift of faith. We can imagine the fervor of our new convert. And in this she exemplifies the consecrated single woman in the world. Edith has written, "Virginity is the highest positive. This means a life of partnership with Christ, marked by radiant joy, an obvious unselfishness, an inner peace which cannot be destroyed by any outer vicissitude, by the rapture with which one lives the Christian life." The deepest and most spiritual concept of purity is to be free of all bonds to oneself or to another; rather, it is to love Christ above all things, not only in mind and heart but in the exercise of daily life. These words of Edith are taken from *Essays on Woman*, a collection of the lectures she gave during these years as a laywoman (Stein, *Essays*, 227, 203).

We are told by the nuns of Speyer about the kind of life she led there. We have said that through baptism, Edith was created a new person. What kind of person was she?

During the years Edith lived at this convent, St. Magdalena, she occupied a small room which was set up like a nun's cell. This room bearing her name is kept in her memory. Near a large cut-off crucifix there is a large portrait of Edith showing her face as mature, very quiet, with a recollected expression; her eyes seem to follow the beholder. Her hands are folded, giving the impression of a prayerful, meditative person. (See further in *Edith Stein zum Gedanken*).

Certainly, Edith spent a great deal of time there in prayer.

She worked and prayed, in keeping with the Benedictine motto. And, indeed, she was very devoted to the Benedictine liturgy, a love which remained with her always. She went to the Benedictine Abbey in Beuron for the holy seasons of Christmas and Easter. The Abbot there, Raphael Walzer, became her spiritual director after Canon Schwind's death. One can see the influence of these three great orders on Edith: the Dominican, the Benedictine and the Carmelite; her friend Father Erich Przywara writes that she is the fruit of all three.

Although her director cautioned her against staying up all night in prayer, she did — many full nights. She prayed much and asked others to pray for her. Her philosophy was that the more you are drawn into the inner life, the more you extend yourself out to the world in order to spend this love for God.

At Speyer, Edith Stein matured in faith. She integrated herself into the lifestyle of the convent. Although she was a well-known figure, her day was like that of her colleagues. The memories of her colleagues and students recall her as a woman of great magnetism; she radiated intelligence and spirit. Her nature was gentle, dignified and distinguished. At the same time, she expressed modesty and humility. She never tried to bring acclaim to herself or to put herself in the limelight.

Her teaching method was fastidious. She gave a lot, knew a lot, and asked for a lot from her students — above all, she asked for discipline. A strict grader, she was nonetheless just and compassionate. Her lectures conveyed knowledge above all things. But Christ was the measure of her action; she brought Him and her faith in Him into the classroom. All that she taught was centered on Christ, the Truth.

Through this empowerment, she became a good and friendly teacher, conducting herself with utter good-will, understanding, trust, and great magnanimity towards these young people. She had one concept which she set as an uncompromising orientation concerning love for neighbor: this was, "spiritual need breaks through every rule." She had no preconceived opinions when people came to her for advice, and, as they had come to her grandmother Adelheid, many did come to Edith. She was particularly interested in the less gifted, shy and socially disadvantaged of her pupils.

Yet she remained objective and detached. Many wrote to her for advice, also. To one young girl, Edith answered that if she really wanted to improve spiritually, she would realize that Edith can't come running to her regardless of her own situation. Surely, she was no pushover! She cautioned another student to cite Edith as source if she does use Edith's article.

On the other hand, she is very humble. To a priest who called her attention to several insufficiencies in the newly published *Truth* which Edith had translated, she answered: "No one could be more convinced than I am that others would have been better qualified for this work.... Perhaps just such an unsuspecting little David had to attack Goliath in order to give stimulus to the heavily armored knights" (Stein, *Self-Portrait in Letters 1916-1942*, 115). Her humor, serenity, patience, and sanctity are clearly evident in these letters.

What is amazing is that during these years, she was able to achieve so much intellectual work in the little cell she occupied. She seems to have been indefatigable. And yet she writes, "I do not use extraordinary means to prolong my workday. I do as much as I can. The ability to accomplish increases noticeably in proportion to the number of things that must be done. When there's nothing urgent at hand, it ceases much sooner. Heaven is expert at economy" (Stein, *S-P*, 72).

But even for her, work became so heavy that she was pressed to give up her post as teacher and to give herself totally to writing and lecturing. Finally, she left Speyer on March 26, 1931.

During the next year, she devoted herself to lecturing and correcting the galleys of her translation of *Truth*. Among other things, she worked on "Act and Potency" which she hoped to make her habilitation, but again she was unable to locate a university position. Finally, in the spring of 1932, she was offered the chair in pedagogy at the German Institute for Scientific Pedagogy in Münster and she accepted.

Here she was to establish a system of Catholic education for the young woman, based on an understanding of her psyche and destiny. Stein's first lectures were on the structure of the person.

And it is now, in 1932, that she goes to France for the Thomistic conference. They tell of a beautiful incident where she sits talking outside the Sacred Heart Church in Montmartre with two of the philosophers, Koyré and a priest, Father Feuling. The latter writes that Edith and Koyré were speaking of Jewish philosophers: Husserl, Bergson, and Myerson. "'He is another of ours' was a constantly recurring phrase. It amused me a little to hear the way Koyré and Edith Stein, speaking of Jews and Jewish matters, would simply say 'we'. I had a vivid impression of that blood-brotherhood which was so strong in Edith, as formerly in St. Paul.... Then I was a little naughty, and asked with a serious air, 'And where are you banishing *me?*' They looked at me in great concern and asked 'Are you one of us, too?' until I assured them of the contrary" (Posselt, 111).

During this period at Münster, Edith took a course especially designed for her by a young Johannes Quasten, the priest who was to become the patristics scholar of our century. She apologized to him for not knowing enough Latin and Greek, and this was just after the appearance of her translation of *Truth* from the Latin. The course he gave to her was the educational doctrine of St. John Chrysostom, which of course Edith was most interested in for her work. Together they read his tract on "Educating Young Children."

At Münster, Edith was experiencing a growing difficulty living in the world, because she was reaching more and more for solitude and the contemplative life. She had an uneasy feeling that she might be making her colleagues a bit uncomfortable.

She is gladdened by the assurance from her friend, Mother Petra, that wearing a habit is not necessarily a prerequisite for the religious life. To another religious friend, Sister Adelgundis, Edith writes of Thérèse of Lisieux: "My impression was simply that there the life of a human being has been formed entirely, from first to last, only and exclusively by the love of God. I know nothing more sublime, and I would wish to have as

much of that as possible in my own life and in the lives of all
who are near to me" (*S-P*, 137).

She lived a Eucharistic life. She spent hours before the
tabernacle: "Dogmatically, I believe the matter is very clear: the
Lord is present in the tabernacle in his divinity and in his humanity. He is not present for his own sake but for ours: it is his
delight to be with the 'children of men'. He knows, too, that,
being what we are, we need his personal nearness. In conse-
quence, every thoughtful and sensitive person will feel attracted and will be there as often and as long as possible" (*S-
P*, 114).

Again, "Whoever seeks to consult with the Eucharistic
God in all her concerns, whoever lets herself be purified by the
sanctifying power coming from the sacrifice at the altar, offering herself in this sacrifice, whoever receives the Lord in her
soul's innermost depths in Holy Communion cannot but be
drawn ever more deeply and powerfully into the flow of divine life, incorporated into the Mystical Body of Christ, her
heart converted to the likeness of the divine heart" (Stein, *Essays*, 56).

Edith was to need this strengthening. Hitler became Reich
Chancellor in January, 1933. Edith was experiencing growing
difficulties with a small group of students who were Nazi sym-
pathizers. Then an incident occurred early in 1933 when she
was locked out one night by what she thinks was an accident.
She was invited to the home of a colleague to spend the night.
There she heard stories, relayed through the American press,
about the persecution of the Jews.

She writes, "I had indeed already heard of severe mea-
sures being taken against the Jews. But now on a sudden it was
luminously clear to me that once again God's hand lay heavy
on His people, and that the destiny of this people was my own"
(Posselt, 117). Let us remember that Edith had said, after her

baptism she felt Jewish again. She was undoubtedly sure that the Father of Christ was also the Father of Israel.

After Hitler's first economic boycott of the Jews on April 1st, 1933, Edith immediately realized the terrible implications. She decided to seek a private audience with Pope Pius XI to ask him to issue an Encyclical denouncing the anti-Semitism of National Socialism. But first she wanted to get permission to do this from her spiritual advisor in Beuron, where she was going for Easter. On her way there, she stopped at the Cologne Carmel for a Holy Hour on the Eve of First Friday. She writes,

> I spoke to our Savior and told Him that I knew that it was His Cross which was now being laid on the Jewish people. Most of them did not understand it; but those who did understand must accept it willingly in the name of all. I wanted to do that, let Him only show me how. When the service was over I had an interior conviction that I had been heard. But in what the bearing of the cross was to consist I did not yet know (Posselt, 118).

She went on to Beuron. She had already been informed that a private audience with the Pope was not possible. So she wrote a letter to the Holy Father, cautioning that what would happen to Jews would happen to Catholics as well. The Abbot took the letter and relayed it to the Vatican that month. In reply, Edith received a blessing for her and her family.

Her last lecture before this Easter holiday had been on February 25th. When she returned to Münster, she found that her teaching position was gone. The Institute was Catholic, and they did invite her to stay for research during the summer. The crisis in her life, as for all in Germany, escalated. Looking back at that time later, she writes to a friend: "'We know that for those who love him, God turns everything to the good' (Rm

8:28). That phrase I quoted from the Letter to the Romans afforded me the greatest comfort and joy during the summer of 1933 in Münster, when my future was still shrouded in total darkness. Never have I prayed the Divine Office of the Martyrs, which recurs so frequently during the Easter cycle, with greater fervor than I did at that time" (*S-P*, 235).

Now she wondered if, after almost twelve years since her baptism, she might not now be free to enter the religious life. On the 30th of April, she went to St. Ludgeri Church where they were observing thirteen straight hours of devotion to the Good Shepherd. She promised herself not to leave until she had made a decision. She writes, "As the final blessing was given, I received the Good Shepherd's consent" (Posselt, 120).

She knew now that she had to carry the cross laid on the Jews and that she had to share their destiny. She knew that she had to spend her life in the prayer of expiation for the sins being shed and for the safety of the humanity she so loved. Carmel was the place for her. Teresa was the final inspiration which had carried her into the Church. But to Edith, Carmel excels as an Order because of its joyous reception of the Crucified Christ.

Perhaps at the time of her entry, Edith was not aware of the Jewish ancestry of St. Teresa of Avila. Although it was not spread abroad, the Carmelites did know of it. Teresa's paternal grandfather was Juan Sanchez (1440-1507), a wealthy textile merchant who lived in Toledo. After converting to Christianity, he reneged and raised his sons in Judaism. Remember, this was the time of the Inquisition. Offered an opportunity for absolution, he confessed to heresy and apostasy. For penance he was compelled to walk each Friday for seven weeks, wearing the yellow tunic of the Judaiser. Teresa's father at the age of four walked with him.

This was in 1484. Teresa's grandfather avoided bankruptcy but he was ruined socially. Although canon law stipulated that baptism is irrevocable, there was such stigma attached to Judaism that the conversos could not act as public officials, members of religious orders, students at a university, or even tax collectors. Her grandfather moved to Avila. His wife was of pure stock, called Old Christian, and he attached her name to his, becoming Juan Sanchez de Cepeda. And in 1500, his purchase of a certificate of pure blood allowed him to take on the status of a nobleman. He was able to arrange marriages for his sons with daughters of Old Christian families, Teresa's mother among them.

Whether Edith knew all this before or after her entry into Carmel, it must have occurred to her that the persecution of the Jews in Spain in the 15th century resembled that of National Socialism.

But now a real agony awaited Edith. To her mother, conversion itself was a problem, for Augusta believed that one should stay in the faith into which one is born. Edith was to be home for two months before entering Carmel, and her family had to be told. Our reserved Edith had only now told one or two persons of her plans.

When Edith returned home, she asked her mother to share memories with her: memories of the Stein family life, of her own Courant family as a young girl, of her husband's parental line, and of their entire family life as community. Edith had decided to write all this in order to present a true picture of Jewish humanity to combat the current Nazi caricature of the Jews. This provided the beginning of Edith's autobiography of her youth, *Life in a Jewish Family.*

Those days must have been a time of tender bonding for Edith and Augusta, these two women who loved each other so deeply. But the joy and peace were shattered quickly. Two weeks after her return, her mother said to her, "What are you going to do with the sisters in Cologne?" "Live with them," Edith answered. This was met by "desperate resistance." For her mother, it was the worst thing possible that could ever happen. Not only did this agony appear as an "inconceivable cruelty" at the very time that Hitler was persecuting the Jews; but now that Augusta was 84 years old and no longer traveled, she knew she would never see her child again.

The other family members, except for Rosa, were also aghast. Even her little niece Susel, aged 12, meeting her alone, confronted her with, "Why are you doing this now?" (Posselt, 129). Edith spoke to her as to an adult, explaining that she was not abandoning her Jewish heritage, that she was still Jewish, that nothing was changed between them; and the convent walls would not protect her from any persecution against the Jews. Susel writes that they all continued to love her, but now a rift separated them.

The pain of Edith's family was her cross. For her, it was a "deep abyss" separating her from her usual inner peace. A few days before she left her home forever, she wrote to a friend, Gertrud von le Fort: "You will help me, won't you, to beg that my mother will be given the strength to bear the leave-taking, and the light to understand it" (*S-P*, 158).

But Edith knew that "...suffering borne in union with the Lord is his suffering, incorporated in the great work of salvation and made fruitful therein." She had chosen to enter Carmel for this work. Her family did not understand that her love for them and for all the Jews was now separating them.

Edith's last day with her family was her forty-second birthday, October 12, 1933. The next morning, Edith went as usual at 5:30 for the first Mass at St. Michael's Church. At breakfast, her mother could not eat; she started to cry. Edith went to her and held her until it was time to go. Her noble mother kissed her very tenderly, but as Edith left, Augusta wept aloud.

Only Rosa and Elsa saw Edith off to the train. When the train went past their house, no one was at the window waving, as there had always been in the past. Edith writes, "So what I had hardly dared to hope for was now real. There could be no violent access of joy. All that lay behind me was too terrible for that. But I was in deep peace — in the haven of the Divine Will" (Posselt, 131).

CHAPTER 3

From Carmel to Auschwitz: Spirituality of a Saint

The death of the saints is precious in the sight of the Lord." So sings the psalmist.

Three years before Edith became a Carmelite, she had expressed an urgent need to enact an inner "holocaustum"; this was her only answer to conditions she was otherwise power-less to change. When she entered Carmel in 1933, the begin-ning of Hitler's dictatorship, she had assured her niece Susel that she would always be part of the family and the Jewish people; and being behind cloistered walls would not protect her. In fact, after a few years, she was to write "...I always have a lively awareness that we do not have a lasting city here" (S-P, 309), for Hitler had already shut down cloisters, simply turn-ing the nuns on to the street.

Edith had chosen Carmel over the other Orders, and she explains her reasons for this clearly. All persons are united in the Mystical Body of Christ. Because Christ is in His members, our suffering is His suffering continuing in us; we thus share in His redemptive action. This is true for all persons and for all religious life. But it is especially true for the Carmelite, who stands as proxy for the salvation of sinners freely and joyfully.

Edith, after all, was suffering as a born Jewess but also as a German. Father Johannes Hirschmann remembers her words: "Who is expiating for what is happening to the Jewish people because of the German people? Who is turning this horrible guilt to a blessing for both peoples?" (Herbstrith, *Edith Stein* [Topos, 1993], 134).

Here is a fair question. Did Edith Stein deliberately seek martyrdom? Probably not, but she was ready for it. She had chosen her path in imitation of Christ and would go wherever the way opened before her. Let us keep this question in the back of our minds as we pursue her journey.

History of Carmel

Edith had attended her first Mass at Carmel a few months before she entered the convent in Cologne. It was the Vigil of the feast of Our Lady of Mt. Carmel which falls on July 16th. The Introit or Opening Prayer reads: "I led you into the Land of Carmel, that you might eat of its fruits and produce." It is Mary, Edith writes, who planted her Order on the lovely summit of Mt. Carmel and then over all the world. Legend has it that it was the Jewish prophet Elijah who first saw Mary in the form of a cloud over the mountain. He had come about 850 B.C. to do battle for Jehovah against the priests of Baal, as described in 1 Kings 18:17-46. "Karmel" is a Hebrew word meaning orchard, in this case, woodland. The site of his cave is traditionally held to have been on the southeast part of the range, which since antiquity has been considered holy, a "land blessed by God" (Jr 50:19).

The earliest historical record stems from the report of a Jew who in 1165 saw a Christian chapel built on that site in honor of Elijah. In 1210, a rule was written by Albert of Vercelli, the Patriarch of Jerusalem, and its basic principles are still followed in Carmel: silence and solitude, renunciation and penance, and a life of prayer. In this early part of the thirteenth century, hermits lived in tiny rooms built on the mountain near the fountain of Elijah; this overlooks the city now called Cayphas. The foundations of a monastery and chapel were found in the excavations of 1958.

An early document dating back to 1370, "The Institutions of the First Monks," provides insight into the Carmelite inner spirit and character still true today. Carmelite perfection lies in imitating Elijah who forsook the material world and practiced poverty, chastity, and obedience. Edith Stein also writes of this early document which presents Elijah as a model of the contemplative life to young religious. "The prophet is told by God to go into the desert and hide in the brook Carith opposite the Jordan, to drink of the brook and to live on the food which God will send him. Thus he becomes the pattern of all those who withdraw into solitude, renounce sin, sensual delights, indeed all earthly things (this is what is meant by 'opposite the Jordan') and hide in the love of God (*Carith* being interpreted as *caritas*)" (Stein, *Science of the Cross*, 8-9).

She writes an entire essay in honor of Elijah which she titled "On the History and Spirit of Carmel." She declares him no mere shadow or legend: he is Carmel's Father and guide, a vital, living tradition of its spirituality. Through her analysis, Elijah becomes the symbol of all spirituality. The section, "Before the Face of God" derives its title from 1 Kings 17:1 where Elijah says, "Just as surely as the Lord, the God of Israel, lives before whose face I stand, this year there will be neither dew nor rain until I give the word."

To stand before the face of God is to watch in prayer because that is what prayer is — the gazing upon God's face. And, Edith writes, this can be a means to contemplation if we think of alertness in prayer as losing oneself in God. To experience the Presence of God in contemplation is a primary aim of Carmelite life. Action lies in prayer, for the salvation of souls derives from contemplation and is directed towards it. Love of God and neighbor, which is perfect charity, enables the will to unite with God's will. Or, as St. Teresa of Avila puts it, the goal is to have no other will but God's and to be ready to suffer all for Him (Jamart, 14-33).

Teresa of Avila, we know, founded the Discalced Carmelites, Edith Stein's Order, in 16th century Spain. The two previous centuries had weakened Carmel's original objectives and discipline. Women had lived according to Carmelite rule for centuries before their formal institution in 1452 by the bull "Cum nulla" by Nicholas V. Carmelites were first settled in the Netherlands and then in different parts of Europe. Teresa of Avila entered this Calced Carmelite order in 1533 in the Convent of the Incarnation, in Avila. In 1562, she founded the first Discalced Carmel, the Convent of St. Joseph, and by the time of her death twenty years later, she had founded fifteen such Carmels.

Mitigations of the original rule, made in 1432 by Eugene IV, which had softened the Carmelite austerity, were removed. The Carmelites now returned to perpetual abstinence from meat and to their yearly fast from September 14, the day of the Feast of the Cross on which they renew their vows, to Easter. More time was now to be spent in daily prayer: two hours of meditation and the Divine Office said in common. Otherwise, silence was to be observed the entire day except for periods of recreation. The cloistered Carmelite's life was one of prayer and penance. She spoke to outsiders only through the grill. She stayed in the same Carmel for life except to found another Carmel.

The Carmelite Vocation

Edith writes a loving tribute to the Carmelite vocation in an essay, "For the First Profession of Sister Miriam of Little Thérèse: July 16, 1940." Mary, the Mother of Christ, gives gifts of grace to her special sisters in Carmel; she chooses the souls she wishes to bring to Christ and covers them with the robe of salvation (which is also the mantle of justice). The Carmelite strives to image God, in the most perfect way, in His holiness and righteousness. Mary is to be followed in her virginal purity, poverty, and obedience. The Bride of Christ surrenders freely to God, and, like little St. Thérèse, will be able to say at the end, "I do not regret that I have given myself to love!" (Stein, *Hidden Life*, 108).

In the essay, "Love for Love: the Life and Works of St. Teresa of Jesus," Edith writes that Carmelite prayer wins grace for souls; the prayer of expiation is the only way to save humanity. How important in this regard are Edith's words three weeks before her death to Jesuit priest, Jon de Nota. "She spoke about the vocation of a Carmelite, how she must represent love in a world of hate" (Herbstrith, *Edith Stein* [Topos, 1993], 128). Her friend, Gertrud von le Fort, echoes this sentiment in her Introduction to *Letters from Marie Antoinette de Geuser, Carmelite in the World*. Le Fort writes that the spirit of Carmel is foreign to our contemporary world and yet is oriented to its deepest needs. It finds in Carmel what is necessary to itself — an intelligibility of its own suffering made worthy through the Carmelite offering — participation in the redemptive suffering of the cross.

Edith also expresses admiration for de Geuser in an admirable essay, "The Prayer of the Church."

What is the prayer of the Church, if not the self-giving of the great lovers to the God who is Love?.... The

limitless loving surrender to God and the divine re-
ward, the perfect and constant union, this is the highest elevation of the heart accessible to us, the highest
stage of prayer. The souls that have achieved this are
truly the heart of the Church; they are filled with the
high-priestly love of Christ. Being hidden with Christ
in God, they cannot do otherwise than radiate into the
hearts of others the divine love with which they are
filled, and so cooperate unto perfecting all into unity
in God, which was and is the great concern of Jesus
Christ. Thus Marie Antoinette de Geuser had understood her vocation (Graef, *Writings*, 43-44).

Edith thus describes prayer as the highest action and "the
highest achievement of which the human spirit is capable" (*HL*,
38). She was herself completely given to prayer and contemplation: her vocation was deeply authentic. As she remembered
others in prayer, she always asked for theirs. Her meditations,
she writes, "are not great flights of the spirit, but mostly very
humble and simple" (*S-P*, 187). In her essay, "The Mystery of
Christmas," she writes that, like the holy babe, we must each
stand before the crib, childlike and trusting in God. Only so can
the penitential spirit of our intercessory prayer unite us to others in the world and in heaven and save souls.

In many works, Edith links the prayer of the Hebrew
Scriptures to that of the New Testament. In "The Prayer of the
Church" Edith reveals knowledge of Jewish as well as of Chris-
tian theology and ritual. She writes that Jesus prayed as a Jew,
and his human prayer is the prototype of the Church's prayer.
The Eucharistic character of prayer is present in the Hebrew
Scriptures: the Hebrew temple imaged creation as it serves and
worships God; while Christ built a temple of the communion
of saints. Christ's high priestly prayer was prefigured in the
Jewish Day of Atonement, when the priest entered the Holy of

Holies to sprinkle the blood of sacrifice and to pray for Israel (Lv 16:16); this was a private room in the temple separated by a veil which only the High Priest could enter on that day. But, she writes of Christ, "His blood is the curtain by which we enter the holy of holies of the divine life" (Graef, *Ibid.*, 45).

Edith often uses imagery and figures of the Hebrew Scriptures for philosophical and theological argument in her major works, *Endliches und Ewiges Sein* and *The Science of the Cross*. It is rather touching that for her fiftieth birthday, her last birthday, the Carmelites prepared a skit, personifying characters from the Hebrew Scriptures, even dressing for the parts. Surely they must have loved her greatly to do so.

Edith's Life as a Carmelite

How did Edith fare as a person in Carmel? Her early confessor, Abbot Raphael Walzer, writes, "She simply ran to Carmel like a child into its mother's arms, blithe and singing, without later regretting this almost blind eagerness even for a moment." He also writes that, when she entered, there was no talk of her continuing her intellectual work. The Cologne Carmel was practically a community of lay sisters; even the choir sisters did the laundry and ironing, the sweeping and scrubbing. But when the Abbot questioned Edith at her clothing some time later, she answered that "she was completely at home in heart and mind" (Posselt, 153-54).

Nonetheless, several sources have described the awkwardness of this intellectual woman in her manual duties; after all, the Stein house had maids for the heavy labor! But we know that she was soon asked by her superiors to return to her work. The first was the autobiography of her youth, *Life in a Jewish Family,* written to honor her mother and to portray the excellence of Jewish humanity.

We remember the agony known by Edith and her family at the time of her final leave-taking in Breslau. Her letters written thereafter clearly evidence the heavy cross which she carried from this suffering — theirs and hers. In time, however, her mother did soften enough to enclose greetings to Edith in the regular letter from Rosa. Edith had initially hoped to be able to transfer to the new Carmel planned for the area of Breslau: Pawelwitz. She indicates reasons why this transfer may not have occurred: she was concentrating in joy over her first profession in April of 1935; in June, the Breslau Carmel was not yet ready and her Superior wanted her to do scholarly work not possible in Breslau. In any case, she makes an almost casual reference in the postscript of a letter in December that the convent in Breslau had been officially dedicated. This Carmel was closed down by the Nazis in 1941.

Most pleasant and informative was an interview with Sister Teresa Margaret, a nun who knew Edith well in Cologne and who was highly involved in her Beatification Process. From her we have an intimate, personal look at our Carmelite, Teresa Benedicta of the Cross. Humility was the most important element of her being. She was very comfortable with the nuns and never spoke of her worldly importance. Edith had already been in the cloister for two years when Sister Margaret asked someone, "Who is she?" "I don't know," she was answered. Discovery of Edith's past as a teacher led to the realization of her importance.

Edith told them stories about her past, and her great sense of humor kept them laughing. She herself would laugh so heartily that tears would stream down her face. She had a natural gift of empathy in personal relationships; she felt another's state of mind and knew what to say in encouragement. Her love and goodness were natural; she had a need to help others.

One December evening in 1936, when the cloister was in total darkness except for the recreation room, Edith missed the

switch on top of the stairs and fell to the bottom. She had broken her ankle but lay there quietly in pain for half an hour. Finally, one of the nuns making the stations of the cross heard a
slight cough — their signal in times of silence. Edith was found
on the floor and quickly sent to the hospital for an x-ray and
cast. There she stayed several weeks until Christmas. Her sister Rosa, who arrived at this time, came to her for instructions
in the faith. Augusta had died a few months before, and Rosa
was free to carry out this desire of many years. On her way back
to the convent, Edith was able to stop for the baptism of her
sister held at a church near the hospital. It was Christmas Eve.

Edith, said Sister Teresa, was artistically inclined. She
loved plastic art, sculpture, paintings and music. She kept small
cards depicting famous paintings. Near the Madonna, she kept
a silver vase made in Japan. She wrote poems and little plays,
but these were all burned when the convent was bombed in
1944.

She preferred to take the private ten day yearly retreat in
her cell away from the community. "I look forward with so
much joy to the silence" (S-P, 171). Her investiture was in April,
1934 when she was able to make a private retreat during Easter. Someone had sent her a large candle and wooden holder
which she was burning. Candlelight and holy silence. What
went on in this sanctified soul during this Holy Week? Her investiture was heavily attended by notables from the academic
and scientific worlds.

Edith was rather thin and delicate; yet she proves the truth
of the words of St. Teresa of Avila regarding the daily schedule: "Our observance of it can be borne quite easily by people
who are not in the least robust, but are really delicate, if they
have sufficient spirituality" (Beevers, 59). The day was offered
up each morning "in union with the unending merits of Jesus
Christ," a practice initiated by the 19th century German Carmelite, Katherina Esser (Lenz, 103). Edith describes the daily

schedule for Lent starting on September 14 until Easter, and then the summer schedule. The summer day starts at 4:30 a.m., the Lenten morning a bit later. Theirs is a steady program of work, prayer and meditation until 9 or 10 p.m., depending on the season. Five hours go by before the dinner is taken, their two meals always of a meatless diet. The time of recreation is spent manually with needlework, packaging altar breads, the making of rope sandals, cleaning vegetables, etc. The hours of the daily Office are recited communally and there are two hours of silent meditation.

Looking at the actual schedule, one must marvel how Edith managed to do all her scholarly work in her free time. She wrote in snatches in the very small pauses in the schedule and did not come to the noon recreation. Her major work, *Endliches und Ewiges Sein*, a very long work, was completed in the period of nine months. I was told that her energy and power of concentration were the gifts of her prayer.

We have referred to many works of Edith written at Cologne. It is natural that her mind and spirit tended towards hagiography, the account of saintly persons. She was particularly concerned with saintly Carmelite women of different countries; these studies reveal her concepts of Carmelite spirituality and of holiness itself. Studies not yet named are on Barbe Acarie (Sr. Mary of the Incarnation), credited with founding Carmel in France in 1604; Thérèse Martin-Guerin (St. Thérèse of Lisieux, the Little Flower), of whom there are loving references scattered throughout her work; the Italian born Anna Maria Redi (St. Teresa Margaret of the Sacred Heart); the 19th century German Katherina Esser (Mother Franceska of the Infinite Merits of Jesus Christ); and, of course, studies on Teresa de Ahumada: "Love for Love: the Life and Works of St. Teresa of Jesus," and another long essay on Teresa of Avila, etc. Some of these hagiographical studies are in translation and can be found in volume 4 of Edith Stein's works, *The Hidden Life.*

Endliches und Ewiges Sein (Finite and Eternal Being), perhaps Edith's most important philosophical work, was the development of a study begun in her Speyer years as a possible habilitation. That early attempt, "Act and Potency," constitutes just one chapter of this work. Her primary concern is as the subtitle suggests, "An Ascent to the Meaning of Being."

Despite an excessive sense of her own shortcomings, Edith confesses that the work is "unabashedly comprehensive." To her friend Hedwig Conrad-Martius, whom she deeply respected as a philosopher, she writes, "If my work deserves the right to exist beside yours at all, it is because it is connected to the tradition. It is an attempt to build bridges (by coupling phenomenology with tradition), and as such it may become useful to some people" (*S-P*, 239-40). That Edith became a bridge builder in many ways we must acknowledge. Many philosophers and theologians of her time highly acclaimed the work: it was indeed of use to them. Yet Edith wrote that she had to be renewed frequently before the tabernacle when her courage "had been crushed by the erudition of other people" (*S-P*, 211). The work was slated for early publication, but because of the political situation, was not issued until after her death. She could have seen it in print by allowing another German nun's name to be affixed as author; but, as in all things, Edith held out for truth.

Edith begins with her personal awareness of self, finite being, in its grasp of Eternal Being. The ego is conscious of its living — of its being thrown into existence. This is recognized as creaturely being requiring One who throws that which is thrown. She builds from this knowledge of the finite "I" to knowledge of being which is founded by an existing Necessary Being.

Her approach in the use of personal consciousness raises the question of the values of which the acting person becomes aware. Between the moment of recognizing that which is no more and that which is not yet in existence, we know the now; and in the moment of clarity regarding one's being and not being in time, we are aware of pure, eternal Being which sustains us. This eternal attraction implies a realm of values. Throughout all her work, Edith uses faith (revelation) as well as natural reason as a source of knowledge. For, "the way of faith gives us more than the way of philosophical knowledge: it gives us the God of personal nearness, the loving and merciful one, and a certainty such as no natural knowledge can give" (*EES*, 58; Graef, *Scholar*, 151).

Edith uses the phenomenological language and method to analyze what is often Thomistic content but which is also based on Aristotle and Plato, St. Augustine, Duns Scotus, and her colleagues Erich Przywara and Hedwig Conrad-Martius. After introductory remarks which include thoughts concerning Christian Philosophy, Edith analyzes concepts of Act and Potency, Essential and Real Being, Form and Substance, Being as Such, the Meaning of Being, the Image of the Trinity in Creation, and the Meaning and Foundation of Personal Being. We will have recourse to some of this in our consideration of Edith Stein's philosophy of the person. Let us be content here in quoting a paragraph which we can accept as explanatory of Edith's strength and courage. She writes,

> The spirit of God is meaning and power. He gives the soul new life and enables it to achieve performances to which a person would not be equal by nature.... In the last resort every meaningful demand which presents itself to the soul with binding power is a word of God.... And if a man willingly accepts such a word of God, he receives by this very fact the divine power to act accordingly (Graef, *Scholar*, 161; Stein, *EES*, 409).

As the political situation worsened, so was Edith's joy subdued. Her family had been struggling to leave Germany. Arno, Elsa, Erna and their families were able to get out just in time. Rosa, Paul and Frieda were still in Germany. In a letter dated October 31, 1938, Edith writes a confession:

> But I trust that from eternity, Mother will take care of them. And (I also trust) in the Lord's having accepted my life for all of them. I keep having to think of Queen Esther who was taken from among her people precisely that she might represent them before the King. I am a very poor and powerless little Esther, but the King who chose me is infinitely great and merciful. That is such great comfort (*S-P*, 291).

Just nine days later, on November 9, the infamous "Night of Crystal" erupted, when thousands of Jews were openly attacked, sent to the camps, their businesses and synagogues burned. The nuns prepared to get her out of Germany before disaster could strike her or them through her. On December 31 she was driven by a friend of the convent to the Carmel in Echt, Holland. On the way out, she stopped for an hour of prayer before the Queen of Peace in the parish church where the present Cologne Carmel now stands. She arrived in Echt on New Year's Eve.

In Echt, Edith was not in the same state of pure childlike joy as she had been earlier. When she first entered Carmel, her soul flew like a bird to its nest (Psalm 11). But is not Carmel a state of being, not a place? We each have prayed "Lord, who shall be admitted to your tent and dwell on your holy mountain?" (Psalm 15). Echt became the place where her sainthood was forged.

The nuns spoke mostly German, for the sisters had come there as a refuge from the nineteenth century *Kulturkampf* (the struggle between church and state) waged by Bismarck. But in 1941, five young Dutch novices entered and the sisters changed over to speaking Dutch, which Edith with her gift for languages mastered quickly. After her arrival, Edith immediately tried to bring Rosa there, who finally did come in the Fall of 1939. Edith prayed for her family, asking all to pray for them. How disappointed she must have been when Erna and the two children had to sail for America (Hans was already there) without being able to see her; it was already February, 1939. In September of that year, Hitler invaded Poland, starting World War II. In the spring of 1940, he was in Holland. Rosa had hoped to become a cloistered nun; now it was deemed best to keep her a Carmelite Tertiary. She acted as sacristan and portress for the Carmel.

An interview with the prioress of the Echt Carmel in 1984, Sister Marie Louise, brought much data to light. She told me that Edith was not melancholy, and although she was very quiet, she always smiled when she was with the sisters. But one could tell she was greatly influenced by the times, for otherwise her face was habitually "*betrübt*", i.e., sad. Sister Marie said that they did not know what went on in the camps, but they felt that something was wrong. They did not expect anything more than hard labor if Edith were arrested. (Here it is necessary to interject a comment made by Father Romaeus Leuven that Edith had been grieved at times in Echt by the often unfeeling, sometimes unfriendly remarks of the nuns regarding Jews [Leuven, 139].)

The prioress reported that Edith tried to help the nuns intellectually. Some of the sisters did manual work, some gardened, and some prayed. Those who worked manually — the lay sisters — were denied library privileges. Edith tried twice to persuade the Prioress to change this but was unsuccessful. We know from her letters that, from the time she first came to Echt, she was interested in obtaining information from other religious communities regarding lay sisters; she was concerned about their training, work and prayer schedules, and participation in communal exercises. And she writes that the existing circumstances are sad because there was no formal concept of the life of the lay sister.

She was in charge of professions and taught Latin to the novices, referring to them as "the little ones" and "the children." One of these novices remembers Edith saying that there is nothing greater than God's love, so that she wanted to keep it in her life and give it to others (Leuven, 138).

The year 1939 has left testimonials of Edith's intense interior life. In March, before the war started — it was Passion Sunday — she wrote to her prioress, offering herself in expiation to the Heart of Jesus so that the Anti-Christ (Hitler) would be overthrown and war averted. In June, she drew up her last will and testament, closing with the following:

> In full submission to God's most holy will, I joyfully accept the death that He has foreordained for me. I pray that He will accept my life and death: for His honor and glory, for all hallowed intentions of the most sacred hearts of Jesus and Mary and of the holy Church; in particular for the preservation, sanctification and perfection of our holy Orders, especially for the Carmels in Cologne and in Echt; as expiation for the unbelief of the Jewish people, so that the Lord will be accepted by His own and His kingdom will come in glory; for the salvation of Germany and for world peace; and finally, for my relatives living and dead and for all whom God has given me, that not one of them will be lost (Herbstrith, *Wahre Gesicht*, 167).

The war broke out in September. During these last years at Echt, Edith was totally centered on the cross. She writes essays commemorating the Carmelite renewal of vows on September 14, the Feast of the Triumph of the Cross. These essays reveal Edith's state of being. In the 1940 essay, "The Marriage of the Lamb," she writes of the Carmelite:

> The spouse whom she chooses is the Lamb that was slain. If she is to enter into heavenly glory with him, she must allow herself to be fastened to his cross. The three vows are the nails. The more willingly she stretches herself out on the cross and endures the blows of the hammer, the more deeply will she experience the reality of her union with the Crucified. Then being crucified itself becomes for her the marriage feast (Stein, *The Hidden Life*, 99).

Her own marriage feast was prepared. She had told Fr. Hirschmann that the suffering of the hated and the pain of the haters must be taken up by those who themselves bear the wounds which hate wields here and now (Herbstrith, *Edith Stein* [Topos, 1993], 134). She and Rosa registered in October 1941, reporting periodically to the Gestapo office in Maastricht, wearing the Yellow Star. Edith was now working on *The Science of the Cross*, a study of the life and work of St. John of the Cross. "That," she wrote, "is a great grace" (*S-P*, 339).

Yet, from her impassioned poetry of that time, we know that she was suffering. Here are some verses, "To God, the Father" (Batzdorff, 81).

> Bless the mind deeply troubled
> Of the sufferers,
> The heavy loneliness of profound souls
> The restlessness of human beings,
> The sorrow which no soul ever confides
> To a sister soul.

And bless the passage of moths (zealots)
at night,
Who do not shun specters on paths
unknown.
Bless the distress of men
Who die within the hour.
Grant them, loving God, a peaceful,
blessed end.

Bless all the hearts, the clouded ones,
Lord, above all,
Bring healing to the sick.
To those in torture, peace.
Teach those who had to carry their
beloved to the grave, to forget.
Leave none in agony of guilt on all the
earth.

Bless the joyous ones, O Lord, and keep
them under Your wing.
My mourning clothes You never yet
removed.
At times my tired shoulders bear a heavy
burden.
But give me strength, and I'll bear it
In penitence to the grave.

Then bless my sleep, the sleep of all
the dead.
Remember what Your son suffered for me
in agony of death.
Your great mercy for all human needs
Give rest to all the dead in Your
eternal peace.

It would seem that the former Red Cross nurse and the Carmelite are weeping together.

Edith's presence at the convent was known, and the well-organized Dutch Resistance Movement offered to get her and Rosa out of the country. Although Bishop Lemmens of Roermond urged them to go into hiding, Edith said no, although she would have gone if so ordered. Many American parachutists who were brought down were helped through the underground. An actual opportunity to escape through a farmer presented itself, but Edith would not accept their help. Again, why?

We know possible answers. She had been waiting for acceptance at Le Pacquier Carmel in Switzerland, and, after the initial delay due to her unwillingness to leave without Rosa, arrangements were finally made for Rosa to be taken to a Tertiary Convent just a few miles from the Swiss Carmel. They had already been told by the Nazi authorities that they could not emigrate until after the war; now they were hoping for special permission to go. Secondly, Edith found it difficult to make another home elsewhere: that would mean being torn twice from her religious community. Also, they had been assured by their superiors that they would be safe as baptized Catholics, according to the latest word of the Gestapo. And, according to her vows, she was obligated to live according to the holy rule as long as it lay in her power. Then, said Sr. Marie Louise, Edith had a real Prussian mentality; she would only go in an orderly, right fashion; subterfuge had no place in her life. Finally, Edith was perhaps clinging to her concept of God's will in her life. She had written once, "The finger of the Almighty writes the lives of his saints so that we read and praise his wondrous works" (Neyer, 163).

Edith was clearly enveloped in God's Holy Spirit. She had written that evil is a created spirit which chooses freely to behave perversely. This can only be counteracted by God's Spirit of Love. One of the last writings before her death was penned on the feast of love, Pentecost of 1942. These are the lines of the first stanza:

> Who are you, sweet light that fills me
> And illumines the darkness of my heart?
> You guide me like a mother's hand,
> And if You let me go, I could not take
> Another step.
> You are the space
> That surrounds and contains my being.
> Without You it would sink into the abyss
> Of nothingness from which You raised it into being.
> You, closer to me than I to myself,
> More inward than my innermost being —
> And yet unreachable, untouchable,
> And bursting the confines of any name:
> Holy Spirit —
> Eternal love!   (Batzdorff, 93)

Her anguish has been totally sublimated by love.

The next month on July 26, a pastoral letter written by the Bishops was read from every Catholic pulpit: it protested the transports of Jews from Holland, and the removal of the Jewish children from Catholic schools, their only remaining means of formal education. In retaliation the next Sunday, August 2nd, the Gestapo arrested every Catholic convert from Judaism. Edith was at community prayer in the chapel. A double clang sounded, a signal that the prioress, Mother Antonio, was wanted in the speakroom. Through the heavy grill, they told her to call Edith Stein. Edith came. Rosa was there also, and the prioress waited by the door, hoping this had to do with the visa for which they were waiting.

The Nazi said to Edith who was behind the grill, "Come out."

"That is impossible," she answered. "I am cloistered."

He repeated, a bit louder, "Come out!"

She said staunchly, "I don't know how. You will have to show me."

The SS officer: "YOU MUST BE READY IN FIVE MINUTES." And to Mother Antonio who, startled, had now come forward, "She must be ready in five minutes!"

Mother Antonio: "That is impossible."

The officer: "Yes, she must."

There was no arguing with this order — everyone knew that. Edith ran to the chapel, knelt, and quietly whispered their need for the sisters' prayers. They took ten minutes to get a few things, while a crowd gathered at the door. As portress, Rosa was well-known and loved, for she was a modest, loving woman. Some knew the importance of Edith Stein in the world of scholarship. A witness, Maria Delsing, has testified that the indignant crowd was murmuring. Rosa was crying, but when Edith said to her quietly, "Come, let us go for our people," Rosa seemed strengthened. A police van was waiting for them. At the corner just yards away, the van made a quick right turn and was gone. As this corner is turned, the cross above the church is sharply visible.

The Amersfoort Camp was situated just twenty kilometers west of Arnheim, not a long ride from Echt. But the driver got lost, and it was late at night when they arrived. The prisoners were roughly treated, pushed, kicked, and beaten and given nothing to eat. Edith and Rosa were brought to Hut #9. A Jewish witness who was later rescued has testified: "The most distressing thing was the condition of the women. It was in this that Edith Stein showed her worth" (Posselt, 229). That was Sunday night. On Monday night, they were put on a train which brought them within four miles of Camp Westerbork, still in Holland. They were obliged to walk about 2 1/2 miles from the platform, carrying their luggage.

Rosa and Edith were steered to Barrack 36 on the foremost left field of the camp.

Edith's first letter to Echt was dated August 4th. She says nothing of the brutality at Amersfoort (in fact, when they had arrived, the whole camp had been standing for days because a prisoner had stolen some bread). Of Westerbork she writes, "We were given a very friendly reception here." (She may have been referring to the Jewish Council which had great authority in running the camp.) Edith writes that they needed ration and I.D. cards, but they were calm and cheerful. "Now we have a chance to experience a little how to live purely from within" (*S-P*, 351). She asks the Prioress to contact the Swiss Consul, and encloses a note to him requesting help so that Rosa and she can cross the border. Rosa also enclosed a brief, brave note to her community.

A letter dated the next day, August 5th, requested that Edith's manuscript of *The Science of the Cross* be retrieved from the Ursuline Convent in Venlo; it was there for typing by a friend of Edith's, Ruth Kantorowitz, who had also been arrested on August 2nd. The kind Jewish Council which had been trying to help had been forbidden to do anything further for them. She counted on the Sisters' prayers. A transport was expected to leave in a few days on Friday. The next day, August 6th, dates her request for warm underclothes and blankets. Rosa had no rosary, and Edith would like the next volume of the breviary. "So far I have been able to pray gloriously!" (*S-P*, 353).

Many witnesses have testified to the abandonment of Edith in her love for the children at the camp, washing and feeding them, cleaning for the mothers, of whom many were lost and distraught. They report her as radiant, consoling all, a saint.

Yet, our intense Edith must have suffered greatly as she looked on that sea of misery. She was not afraid for herself: she had disciplined herself for heavy labor, cold and hunger. But for Rosa, and all the countless others? And finally, she must have realized the enormity of the Jewish persecution, for at the last hour, Edith could not turn her back on them. A friendly Dutch official of the camp, Wielek, published his account of her days at the camp: he writes that he suggested getting a friendly guard to make a last telephone call to prevent Edith and Rosa from being put on that train. Edith smiled and asked him not to. As a baptized Jew, she could not accept the help so impossible to Jews, and if she could not share their lot, her life would be obliterated (Herbstrith, *Edith Stein* [Ignatius, 1992], 186-87).

On the right side of the street to Camp Westerbork, there are now broad grass strips covering the area of the former railway embankment. Over this the prisoners were taken directly from Camp Westerbork to Auschwitz. By the end of 1944, 100,000 Jews were deported over these tracks. During the night of August 6th-7th, the transport left Hooghalen station. It was First Friday and the remembrance of the Feast of the Sacred Heart.

It is recorded that the train carried 987 souls, among which were 120 baptized Jews. I was told by the Director of the Oswiecim Museum (which was formerly the Auschwitz-Birkenau Concentration Camp, German names given to the former Polish territory) that when the train arrived on August 9th, 559 persons dismounted. If the original figure of 987 passengers is correct, it can only mean that either 426 persons were discharged elsewhere, which is highly unlikely since the trains went directly to Auschwitz, or that they perished during the two terrible days of travel on the train.

They were divided into two groups: 264 persons in one group, Rosa and Edith among them, were gassed and burned in a pit that very day. They never entered the camp. They had walked about 15 minutes through a grove where they were told to disrobe and leave their things. They were brought to a white cottage, formerly a farmer's home, where the doors and windows were boarded up for the gassing with Zyklon B. I have always thought that when Edith entered the cottage, she was carrying a small child.

Her labors are over. She climbed the mountain to the top. With Christ, she was nailed to the Cross.

In the Breviary's prayer from the Common of a Martyr, we find St. Augustine's homily on the psalmist's song, "The death of the saints is precious in the sight of the Lord." He writes that, reflecting on what Christ the King of Martyrs has done for us, man cries out "'What shall I give the Lord for all he has given me? I shall take up the cup of salvation....' It is the cup of suffering. 'But are you not afraid you will weaken?' 'No,' they reply, 'Because I shall call upon the name of the Lord.' Blessed are those who have drunk of this cup! Their torments are at an end, and they have taken their place of honor. And so, my dear ones, consider: although you cannot see with your eyes, do so with your mind and soul, and see that *the death of the saints is precious in the sight of the Lord.*"

We have already had occasion to address some of Edith Stein's works, partly in a biographical context. Let us now develop some of the basic themes found in her writings. Here we are in the domain of Christian philosophy and theology.

PART TWO

Writings in Christian Philosophy

CHAPTER 4

Edith Stein's Philosophy of the Woman

The woman as person is Edith Stein's focus as a feminist. She writes that the woman must be fulfilled as an individual person and human being in order to be fulfilled as a woman. Edith beautifully defines human sexuality and marriage as well. Her work is a twofold achievement: her scientific methodology is the product of a true phenomenologist, while the content of her work reveals the Christian philosopher-theologian. Perhaps a century ahead of her time, she has clearly influenced later Church documents.

A Comparison of Philosophies on Woman:
Edith Stein and the Church

Edith was totally devoted to the Church: her belief was absolute concerning the depository of faith, the sacraments, and the beneficent role the Church plays for each of its members and for society in general: this informs her entire philosophy of woman's mission and role. But she was also aware of its human failings.

She writes, "The Church as the Kingdom of God in this world should reflect changes in human thought. Only by accepting each age as it is and treating it according to its singular nature can the Church bring eternal truth and life to temporality" (Stein, *Essays*, 169).

At times, contemporary feminists bring Edith to task for not having been radical enough as a feminist. But when we know the actual state of affairs in both the Church and the society of her time, we realize the tremendous contribution she has made to the cause of women.

At the end of the 18th century, Pope Pius VI quoted Pope Clement XI in a letter regarding intermarriage: "Women's nature is such that it is much easier for them to lead their husbands into error than for their husbands to lead them into truth" (*Matrimony*, 60). But we need not go back that far. Let us go to 1930, when Pope Pius XI issued his encyclical *Casti Connubii*. He writes of "the loyal and honorable obedience of the wife to her husband" (*Matrimony*, 258). He does stipulate that this differs according to the situation, and a woman need not obey if it is against right reason. He quotes Leo XIII who wrote that a woman should obey as a companion, not as a servant, "wanting in neither honor nor dignity," indeed, "a heaven-born love guiding both in their respective duties" (*Woman in the Modern World*, 35-37).

Edith Stein had already started in 1928, two years before this Encyclical, to present her progressive ideas in lectures on the woman. She concurs on this point, the position of the husband as head of the family, and it is a point where radical feminists attack her. But so progressive is her formulation of the personhood of woman, her equality, the complementarity of the sexes, and the restoration of balance between the sexes through redemption that this point loses in significance.

Moreover, her writings openly defy the Nazi tendencies to reduce the woman to the realm of "Church, kitchen, and children." She declares that woman must never lose her prerogative of self-autonomy and free judgment then under Nazi attack. She warns against "that brutal attitude which considers woman merely from the biological point of view; indeed, this is the attitude which characterizes the political group now in power" (*Essays*, 157).

Certainly, she had never accepted the concept of submissiveness for herself, and we suggest that it is a decisive reason why she never could follow through with a romantic attachment. It has been said that Edith was romantically inclined twice, both times involving philosophical colleagues, Hans Lipps and Roman Ingarden. Speaking of her position as Husserl's assistant, she writes to Ingarden in 1918: "Basically, it is the thought of being at someone's disposition that I cannot bear. I can place myself at the service of something, and I can do all manner of things for the love of someone, but to be at the service of a person, in short — to obey, is something I cannot do" (*S-P*, 22). Of course at that time her devotion to the person of Christ was growing, soon to preclude all other attachments. This love would be perfected in total self-abandon, humility, and obedience to Him.

Pope Pius XI wrote that a certain inequality and adjustment between husband and wife are needed for the welfare of the family — the husband, of course, being the head. But Edith writes that man and woman are to complement each other as one hand does the other. She bases this concept on the Hebraic phrase from Scripture "*Eser kenegdo,*" which means "complementary helpmate." Edith writes that man and woman reflect God's image differently according to their nature as man or woman. Thus, humanity is a dual species designed as complementary halves, creating a harmonious humanity together. It is this which gives the sexual relation its own meaning and value.

Her analysis of differential psychology is still most relevant today. She writes, "...woman strives towards the divine perfection more by the harmonious development of all her faculties; man through a more intense development of particular ones" (*Essays*, 188). This results from their different natures, for a woman yearns for a wholeness of being while the man often loses in a development to full humanity because of his drive to excel in a particular specialization. This involves another difference: a woman's main concern is personal relationships while the man's chief concern is the objective work at hand.

But Edith concedes that the individual's own psyche is a determining factor, for many men and women have traits of the opposite sex. Also, she suggests that existing types of men and women do change in a sexual evolution which advances through the generations. She suggests that "the nature of woman, how (she is) suited to her destiny, can admit of modification without her essence being annulled" (*Essays*, 277-78). This could mean that a change in sex roles is not necessarily a change in woman's essence.

Pius XI wrote in *Casti Connubii* that perhaps some economic and social changes have to take place for the wife who works, but, of course, this number of women were best to remain in the minority. Edith also cautioned the young mother to stay home with her small child, for there is no one who can really replace her. The mother is the most important factor in the formation of the child's character, for through her the child learns to obey in joy and love instead of fear. Without her, the child does not as easily develop trust in God and in other persons, considerateness, self-autonomy, and responsibility.

But Edith also advocated the authenticity of the working wife. If severe economic hardship or high personal talents exist, then right reason dictates that the woman should work outside the home; this does not violate woman's nature or grace. But always, the woman is to provide safe care for her children and never relinquish her primary role as mother or wife. Natural law dictates that her natural vocation is that of spouse, companion, and mother.

God's mandate was given to both sexes: to understand the world, to possess and enjoy it, and to continue its creation through purposeful activity. The gifts enabling man and woman to do so differ. The man is gifted more with bodily strength, the capacity for abstract thought, and for independent creativity. His primary vocation is that of ruler; his role as father is secondary. He is to sustain and protect his wife, guide and encourage his children. The wife must ensure that the father bonds with the family and does not alienate himself from them through excess in his work.

But for the woman, motherhood is her primary role; that of ruler is secondary. And should she work, it is she who is now obligated to guard against the danger of loosened bonds with her children due to an over-zealousness for her career.

It is woman's spiritual essence of motherliness which also provides her identity in professional, public, and religious life. The woman is acutely needed in the marketplace for this very gift of "motherliness." In fact, Edith Stein saw woman as the bearer of God's tenderness: she went so far as to refer to the Holy Spirit as the femininity of God — a truly avant garde concept for her day. She writes, "In this *womanhood* devoted to the service of love, is there really a divine image? Indeed, yes. A ministering love means *assistance* lent to all creatures in order to lead them toward perfection. But such love is properly the attribute of the Holy Spirit. Thus we can see the prototype of the feminine being in the Spirit of God poured out over all creatures" (*Essays*, 200). And woman reflects God's compassion in her motherly concern for the material as well as spiritual needs of others.

Woman's unique nature and intrinsic value are needed by the community. Her drive to develop all her faculties as intended by God, and to help others in the same way, holds great potential for the development of the present generation and for the future of the human race. "Certain maladies of modern culture," she writes, "such as the dehumanization of the person, fragmentation, and the one-sided development of certain faculties leading to the atrophy of others may be cured through recourse to the intrinsic value of woman" *(Essays, 39)*.

Woman is by nature especially gifted to surrender totally to God. Religious education is therefore the basis of her education because the factor of grace must enter into her formation. The ideal image of woman's soul is that it be expansive, quiet, clear, warm, self-contained, empty of self, and mistress over itself and the body.

Her concepts, we would think, explain the preponderance of woman in houses of worship. But this also explains the natural gift of woman to join religious Orders or, in fact, to serve God as a single consecrated woman in the world. And her philosophy explains the mystic level attained by so many women, religious and secular.

In his encyclical *Casti Connubii*, Pius XI develops St. Augustine's concept of the blessings of marriage as offspring, as fidelity between the married couple, and as sacrament. Edith lauds this encyclical; she writes that the Catholic philosophy of marriage which it outlines is the only safeguard to protect marriage from crumbling as an institution. In their day, the promiscuity was already frightening. However, she also writes, "But the concept of marriage on a Catholic foundation must be further elaborated...." She asks for "the setup of a genuinely Catholic broad-minded approach to marriage and sexuality"; this would include sex education for the young — boys and girls. She stresses that early preparation for puberty is vital; at this time, youth can be led to the "profound and sacred meaning" of being a man or woman and child of God *(Essays, 150)*.

There is no doubt that Edith Stein anticipated many of the changes within the Church and foreshadowed the more recent developments regarding its views on women. A new tone was already voiced by Pope Pius XII in 1946 when, speaking of woman's new evolutionary position outside of the home — her new professional and public life — he refers to its advantages as well as its perils. This tone is wonderfully heightened in *Pacem in Terris*, when Pope John XXIII writes: "Since women are becoming ever more conscious of their human dignity, they will not tolerate being treated as merely material instruments, but demand rights befitting a human person both in domestic and public life.... Thus in very many human beings the inferiority complex which endured for hundreds of thousands of years is disappearing, while in others there is an attenuation and gradual fading of the corresponding superiority complex which had its roots in socioeconomic privileges, sex or political standing" (Higgens, 3).

This is not the place for an historical coverage of the slowly improving stance of the Church regarding women. Certainly we must acknowledge the contribution made by Pope Paul VI. But let us proceed to our beloved Holy Father, John Paul II. In his philosophical work, he clearly shows the influence of Edith Stein, particularly on the questions of the sexes and the person. As young Professor Wojtyla at the University of Lublin, our Holy Father had familiarized himself with Edith's work and often suggested her writings to his students as rich material for doctoral studies.

In his apostolic letter *Mulieris Dignitatem* (On the Dignity and Vocation of Women), John Paul II evidences Edith's chain of ideas. He writes that men and women are equal, for their love is a "communion of persons." He traces their original relationship as lost in the Fall and restored through Christ's redemption. He echoes some of Edith's most basic themes, including the complementarity which exists between man and woman based on the original order of creation. She writes, God's intention that they be harmonious is thwarted by the entrance of sin: the person is no longer a child of God; the body wages war against the soul; and the battle of the sexes begins.

It is through the Fall that the submission of woman to man is imposed. But this runs counter to the original harmony created by God which will be restored by redemption.

For God intends the restoration of pure nature (which is the whole person) through Christ. Each person's significance as a person comes from reflecting God's image in a particular way. And it would follow that the restoration of pure nature would restore the initial equality and balance between the sexes. Indeed, Edith writes of the husband and wife, "the more redemption is personally adopted, the more it makes possible a harmonious collaboration and an agreement concerning the allotment of vocational roles" (*Essays*, 80-81).

We will at a later time pursue Edith's influence on our Holy Father regarding his philosophy of the person.

Let us not forego mentioning the American Bishops' first draft, "Partners in the Mystery of Redemption" where one finds an actual reiteration of her themes: men and women as partners in personhood, relationships, in society, and in the Church. We read here of the dignity and equality of each human being, the complementarity of the sexes, the necessary union of man and woman to reflect the full image of God, their partnership in the mystery of redemption, the justice of equal opportunity in educational, professional, and public life for women, etc. Yet we can also recognize that the Church has as yet not caught up with Edith's liberality of thought.

One of the important problems in the Church is treated carefully by Edith Stein: the question of the priesthood for women. She voices two views. First, she supports woman's fight for activities in an "ordained church ministry" and asks if this could be the first step toward the priesthood for women.

She writes, it is tradition, not dogma or canon law, which precludes such priestly activity, for the woman's natural vocation is seen in the home. Yet there has been no actual definition "ex cathedra" on woman's place in the Church. She emphasizes that the call to Catholic action is for women as well as men: she envisions an increase of women in Church duties and asks if these greater numbers might in time change canon law. She cites the important presence of women in early Church history as they worked an "intense apostolate as confessors and martyrs" (*Essays*, 83). The fact that there were once consecrated deaconesses may indicate the possibility of a return in that direction.

But Edith Stein voices a second view, objectively presenting the other side of the question. Christ came as the *son of man*, and perhaps for that reason, He chose only men as His apostles. This is basic to her view that Christ's exclusion of women among His apostles was meant for all time, not just His own. She adds that she personally does not think that women will ever be priests. Yet, she seems to leave the question somewhat open.

Edith refers to the question of the priesthood for women as a mystery. She writes, Christ did not choose Mary as an apostle, yet she and other women were bound in intimate love with Him. She suggests that God may grant woman the special grace of a loving union by His side rather than the empowered authority of the priest. And let us remember that she emphasizes the boundless ministry open to women through the Holy Spirit.

Edith Stein's Contribution to the Education of Women

Edith had become involved in feminist issues as a young Jewess: she had been an early suffragette, a member of the Prussian Association for Women's Rights, the Union for School Reform, etc. We also know that in the 1920's, she became philosophically involved in the nature and vocation of woman because, as a Catholic, she was teaching young Catholic women.

Now, in 1932, Edith was attempting to construct an independent, Catholic educational system for girls at the German Scientific Institute for Pedagogy in Münster. This construct was to be based on the nature and destiny specific to woman, using subject matter and vocational training geared to the feminine nature. Teachers would be women who would focus on the professional opportunities and ethos of the woman.

There was at that time no such system in Germany. Although some schools were conducted by particular religious denominations, education was controlled by the state. Not only were the teaching methods and curricula of the Catholic schools state controlled, but the teachers were apt to be secular or non-Catholic because there were not enough Catholics qualified to teach.

In order to recognize Stein's unique contribution as a feminist and educator, let us place her historically in the European Feminist Movement as it grappled with the problem of education for women. She was born at a time of crisis and excitement concerning this issue. The development of her own personal character and destiny was such that she was impelled to give herself in answer to that need.

The year 1891, when Edith Stein was born, also marked the first admission of German women to a university education; however, this was only as auditors. Their first actual admittance was in 1901, but, again, only in a special category. Their first general admittance to regular matriculation in Prussia was in 1908, so that Stein's entrance into the University of Breslau in 1911 was at the very onset of university rights for women.

We remember her many unsuccessful attempts at various universities to complete a habilitation, i.e., the writing of a second doctoral dissertation while teaching at a university. At the time this was not generally open to women. She finally wrote to the Prussian Minister of Culture, asking that women be allowed to achieve an habilitation, and this did follow in 1920. She writes at that time, "That circular to the universities regarding the habilitation of women was due to my request, certainly, but I promise myself very little by way of results. It was only a rap on the knuckles for the gentlemen in Göttingen" (*S-P*, 44). A feisty lady!

The universities were slowly welcoming women, but college preparatory schools were refusing to admit girls! In 1914 there were in Prussia 540 high schools preparing boys for the university and only 43 for girls (Anthony, 35). The high school girl of the early 20th century was expected to be docile, manageable, have pretty manners, and know next to nothing of mathematics, history and the natural sciences. No attention was paid to the girl's unique nature and individual judgment. Edith referred to this product of 19th century education as "an *ornament of the domestic hearth*" (Stein, *Essays*, 166).

The secular Feminist Movement made the first stab at combating the masculine system. However, it fought to incorporate into girls' schools the curriculum prescribed for boys, for in their zeal, the feminists of the time were denying that there were psychic differences between the man and the woman. But some attempt was made to consider their feminine ethos after 1919, when general school attendance for girls up to eighteen years of age was finally authorized.

Also in 1917, there had emerged a new type of Women's Schools which prepared women for new fields: nursing, social services, government posts, arts, technology, etc. Even bar admittance was granted in 1919; yet we recall sadly that Edith's attempt to get a university post in 1918 failed primarily because there were few women teaching on the university level. Stein, therefore, was trying to meet the needs of a concrete, practical situation in crisis regarding both secondary education in general and Catholic education in particular.

She was considered the woman best suited to meet "the

woman's problem" on the basis of Catholic thought. We have noted that it was the Jesuit philosopher-theologian Erich Przywara who set up a lecture tour for her in 1928. This was to continue into 1933 as she lectured throughout Europe for various associations of Catholic women and Catholic women teachers. These groups became the Catholic Women's Movement, a movement respected by the Church. She became its theorist and was considered its "voice." Her lectures constitute the text *Die Frau*, published in translation as *Essays on Woman*.

Dr. Lucy Gelber, German editor of *Die Frau*, writes that, when Edith began her analysis of woman's psyche, little was available to help her from a psychological perspective and nothing from the religious point of view (*Essays*, 15). Her early work in psychology combined with her experience in education, philosophy, and theology to render her a master in education.

This expertise was much needed. A 1930 dictionary of contemporary education reveals how great the need was for the scientific structure which Stein was asked to create in Münster just two years later (Spieler, 1180). In her essay, "Basic Foundations of Woman's Education," Stein presents her entire concept. What was needed was a transfer from the sheer memorizing of academic material to the harmonious workings of the student's faculties and a development of personhood.

We have seen that the focus in secondary schools had been masculine and non-Catholic. Now Edith urged Catholic women "to work for a specifically *Catholic* and *feminine* approach to girls' education." She reminded them that the education of youth had always been a concern of the Church, and that secular, masculine domination was a modern development. She urged them to join other Catholic groups interested in the cause; however, she also encouraged them to cooperate with secular feminist movements because the education of girls "is specifically a feminine responsibility." But whereas the non-Catholic Feminist Movement was based on a "philosophical and political Liberalism," the Catholic Women's Movement must be founded "on faith and a Catholic world view" (*Essays*, 171).

Edith's focus, therefore, as both educator and feminist, was to form young women who would be anchored as spiritual persons in order to function at their highest level in the home, society, or convent. It is fitting then that we reflect on her philosophy concerning the young woman. (Some of this content relates to the formation of human personhood regardless of gender and can readily apply to the young man as well.)

Edith Stein's Message to the Young Woman

She begins one of her essays analyzing women with the sentence, "We are trying to attain insight into the innermost recesses of our being; we see that it is not a completed being but rather a being in the process of becoming..." (*Essays*, 88). She is applying this concept of potential not only to women as a species but to each girl in her process of formation.

Stein loved the young. Her work as an educator remains for the young of all generations. She taught high school and college students; she addressed assemblies of college graduates and teachers. Were Stein directly addressing young women here, you would feel her great love. I would like to convey now, based on her writings, some of the things she might voice in this love.

First, she might say, "This is the springtime of your life. God has planted in each of you His image in a unique way. This is the meaning of your life: to bring that image to a total and pure development. To do so, He asks that you live in the hand of God, that you live purely and love purely."

We each have certain qualities and talents which are predetermined, and it is our responsibility to help bring these qualities within us to perfection. We are equally responsible for striving towards God and cooperating with His grace to perfect our innermost depths — our spiritual life. Each individual person must discover her unique gifts and freely give herself to the goal of education. This goal is the formation of the unique individuality of each soul.

The feminine self is to be understood in terms of an Aristotelian-Thomistic concept: i.e., "Form is the spiritual essence of the body." It is this essence, this form which gives your feminine body its shape and structure, your feminine psyche, and accounts for your differences from the man! He has his own form!

"All created being is an analogy to divine Being" (*Essays,* 182); i.e., you are an image of your Creator. The excellence of yourself as a human being is that you are aware of yourself and can act freely to develop to full personhood as that image of God. But God has already empowered you within. God has already instilled in you the pursuit of Himself. And it is vital that you learn to dwell within your interior self, to be the mistress of your own soul, i.e., to be self-contained, to be in charge. This quality of self-possession gives you excellence as a human being — in that you are like your Creator. And understand clearly — in this process of your being and becoming, God Himself gives you a power to progress from potentiality to actuality, to be what *you* are supposed to be, to go *your* way, and to perform *your* special contribution in work.

Love hastens us to give back to God our own gift — the gift of self as perfectly formed as He has given us to form. This presupposes that you understand yourself and other persons, society as a whole, and your particular relationships within that cosmos. It means you understand yourself as a child of God and your relationship to Him.

You need to understand with the heart as well as your mind because your essence is to love and to love purely. Only pure love can keep you from ambivalence, even turmoil, regarding your own personhood and your relationships. It is part of your nature as a woman to be totally involved in what you do, and this cannot be if your being is in conflict with itself. And you cannot achieve that self-containment of being, which is your excellence, if you live in a dependency on others for the fulfillment of your being. God alone can fully answer your need for love, and for that, He asks for your love.

He also asks that we love others for His sake. If we love them for ourselves, we try to possess them and make use of them. What is needed instead is to strive for a wholeness of personhood ourselves and to help others to that same fullness of being.

Many women today are not whole in their personhood. How can they be "healthy cells in a sick society" if they themselves are confused and sick? The weaknesses of many women of the 20's and 30's are the same weaknesses of the 90's: i.e., an excessive drive for self-importance, "a mania to know everything and thereby to skim the surface of everything and to plunge deeply into nothing" (*Essays*, 257). This can lead to frustration as easily as the hyper-feminism which seeks compensation for one's own inadequacies by "a perverse desire to penetrate into personal lives, a passion of wanting to confiscate people" (*Essays*, 257). These tendencies are the very opposite of a woman's basic drive to achieve a totality of being and a self-containment of that being.

How can we attain this totality of being? First of all, by thoroughly objective work which gives a freedom in personhood, a way for self-development and self-control. Work provides the opportunity to exercise our feminine essence — to put a feminine stamp on our activity no matter what activity, what profession, or what state of life in which we are engaged. This means that our being is true to our unique nature and our intrinsic value as women.

For an understanding of our unique feminine nature, let us look to the pure love and spiritual maternity of Mary. This spiritual maternity is the core of a woman's soul. Wherever a woman functions authentically in this spirit of maternal pure love, Mary collaborates with her. This holds true whether the woman is married or single, professional or domestic or both, a Religious in the world or in the convent. Through this love, a woman is God's special weapon in His fight against evil. Her intrinsic value is that she is able to do so because she has a special susceptibility for the works of God in souls — her own and others. She relates to others in His spirit of love.

Exercising this feminine stamp on the job prevents her from being harmed as a woman in what has heretofore been a masculine world. Only so can she satisfy her own goals and needs and prevent violation of her own psyche and spirit. Wherever woman has incorporated her authentic feminine approach, no matter what profession — this becomes a legitimate feminine profession even if in the past this has been mostly a masculine occupation. Stein does believe that there are particular occupations in which women can excel because of their feminine drive to build and heal, such as that of teacher, doctor, social worker, lawyer, and politician. But as a woman, you can sustain and counsel all persons in need. Through your warmth and empathy, you can relieve the anguish of the human heart, not only those of your own family and friends, but of all who are burdened, in imitation of Mary, Mother of Mercy.

It is supernatural aid which will enable you to have the right outlook regarding your own person and your relationship to others. Through prayer and the Sacraments, we are empowered to carry God's values into society. We do so as co-responsible members of this society. For each of us is responsible for all of our brothers and sisters in the human family, and cosmic humanity is responsible for each individual.

This can only be achieved by the person who attains the

highest level of prayer in surrender to God, for personhood is freed and sublimated in a lasting union with God. This surrender must of necessity entail a detachment from self and from others. In this detachment, we win the resurrected, divine life within, a life of impersonal, or pure love. You can be the Spouse of Christ whether you are married, single or Religious. This impersonal love is the deepest meaning of purity, and the love of Christ becomes "the inmost formative principle of a woman's soul" (*Essays*, 56). She becomes "ready to serve, compassionate, to awaken and foster life" (*Essays*, 52). This corresponds perfectly to the professional ethos demanded of woman. The face of the earth could be changed by such women.

Women have a special affinity and joy in beauty and goodness. You must be able to judge what is true against what may seem to be true. Knowing exactly *why* something is good or beautiful, you will not simply go along with peer pressure. It is no longer possible for a young person to stand on the sidelines, to exist in apathy, or to simply go along with the tide of peer opinions. It is the young of this generation who must grow to overcome the plagues of promiscuity, abortion, broken families, drugs and violence of every kind. This is a world of broken relationships between people, and between the human being and God. You can, by a fearless faith, help to fight the evil which is everywhere.

Knowledge of the virginity and spirituality of Mary means everything. Purity is the important ingredient because you are surrounded by so much impurity. Everything starts with Mary. Just as Christ was born through her surrender to the Holy Spirit, so from each woman's free gift of self to God there can come order from disorder.

Woman has a special ease and gift with words. Certainly this is borne out by test statistics. Even in the case of young children, girls seem to outdo the boys in ability to express themselves. Of course, this power can become perverse, a destructive tendency, when volubility is combined with possessiveness. But, a study of logic, grammar and languages leads to the right use of speech. This is a means of personality development, a release and revelation of the life within: "What one cannot express remains dark and gloomy in the soul, and whoever is unable to express himself is imprisoned in his own soul; he is unable to liberate himself and cannot relate to others" (*Essays*, 231). What goodness women could wield through their gift of eloquence!

It is imperative that women have contact with all achievements of the human mind through a study of the written word, arts and humanities. A study of multiple cultures and disciplines is necessary for the development of intellect and objectivity. Your mind is made to understand and to enjoy the different works of all cultures and it needs this contact for full development. Every artist is a mouthpiece of God.

Actually, the girl should be placed in contact with all human achievements because these reflect the mind of God as well as the human mind. Art awakens joy in beauty and stimulates talents. Mathematics and natural sciences train the girl in thought; this is necessary since the intellect is primary in the formation of personality. Philosophy and religious training serve the metaphysical tendency. Studies in anthropology and pedagogy are essential in girls' education because *"human development* is the *most specific and exalted mission of woman"* (*Essays*, 220).

The most vital of all professions for women is the teacher who exemplifies spiritual maternity par excellence.

Again, we need women who dedicate their lives to the purpose of educating youth, women who are fully aware of the teachings of the faith and of its historic background. Their intent will be to form a generation which is happy in faith and strong in spirit, a generation which is prepared and ready for both marriage in the highest and purest sense and for virginity dedicated to God according to the model and under the guidance of the Virgin Mother (*Essays*, 268).

We as women are working in the vineyard for our own redemption as a species as well as serving for the redemption of humanity. The question is, are we to delve deeper and deeper into confusion or forge our way up to the concept of pure womanhood as it first existed in the heart and mind of God? Woman is not meant to be identical with man but complementary to him. Could it be that radical feminists are erasing the mystery of woman and hence the romance between the sexes? Let us give ourselves in pure love so that God's grace can work in these fearful times to add new stature, new poetry to human nature which has become so fearfully denigrated and polluted.

Women can help to make a new world and a far better one. But let us not look to men as the standard but only to God who grants us full freedom as women to help create this world. What we become and what we create call to us like the light in a towerhouse, beckoning us out of the violent storms in which so many women and their families are thrashing about today.

Finally, Edith Stein might say: "God bless each one of you!"

1. Edith Stein, Sr. Teresa Benedicta of the Cross (1938)

2. Family portrait of the Stein family (1895); (l-r) back row: Arno, Else, Siegfried (father), Elfriede (Frieda), Paul; front row: Rosa, Auguste (mother), Edith, Erna. Edith's father Siegfried died in 1893. His picture was superimposed on this photo.

3. The Stein family's house in Breslau (now Wroclaw)

4. (l) Erna Stein; (r) Edith Stein

5. Edmund Husserl

6. (l-r) back row: Frau Platau, Frau Dorothea Biberstein, Frau Auguste Stein (Edith's mother); middle row: Rose Guttmann, Paul Berg, Erna Stein, Hede Guttmann, Elfriede (Frieda) Stein Tworoger; front row: Edith Stein, Lilli Platau (the baby is Erika Tworoger, Elfriede's daughter), Rosa Stein

7. (l-r) back row: Sophie Mark, Frau Guttmann, Edith Stein; middle row: Erna Stein, Rose Guttmann, Lilli Platau; front row: Hans Biberstein

8. Edith Stein (seated, left end of the table) as a Red Cross nurse at the Mährisch-Weisskirchen hospital for contagious diseases, 1915

9. Edith Stein, c. 1916

10. Edith Stein with a nephew
(1921)

11. Auguste Stein (Edith's
mother), c. 1925

13. Edith Stein, c. 1925

12. Edith Stein, c. 1925-1930

14. Edith Stein during her year at the German Institute of Scientific Pedagogy at Münster, 1932-33

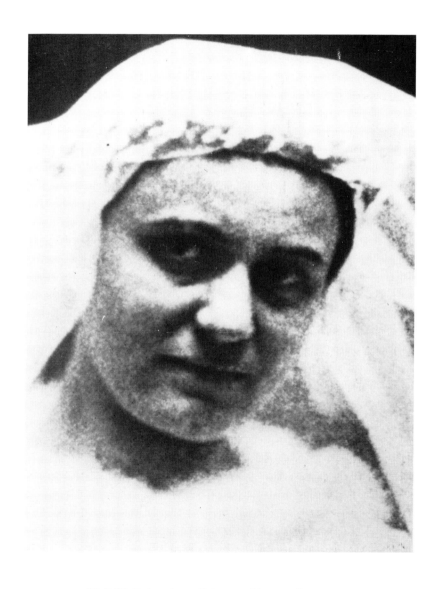

15. Edith Stein at her religious vestition, April 15, 1934

CHAPTER 5

Edith Stein's Philosophy of the Person

I t really is no surprise that this magnificent woman, Edith Stein — who was to give herself as expiation for the oppressor, in solidarity with the oppressed — was drawn as a young woman to write her dissertation *On the Problem of Empathy*. This first study holds the seeds of themes developed in her later work. The two phases — phenomenology and Christian philosophy — differ greatly. For this presentation, I have tried to integrate some of the vast treasury of concepts concerning personhood found throughout her work into a meaningful whole.

The Early Phase — Phenomenology

Edith's major professor, Edmund Husserl, had used the term "empathy" to express the knowing experience shared by two persons, i.e., "intersubjectivity." It is only this process, he believed, that allows us to know the world objectively. In Edith's study, which Husserl acknowledged to be quite independent, she examines the nature of empathy in order to understand person as a physical-psychical-spiritual entity. But in this analysis, she reveals not only the process of self-knowledge but knowledge of the "other" person as the basis of human relationship and social community.

In her early and later work, Edith stresses that spirit is the essence of personhood. But we shall see that she uses the term "spirit" differently before and after her conversion. True to her calling as a phenomenologist, this early study is mostly a philosophy of consciousness. She uses the word "God" only four times and that briefly. In the later work, the element of grace is added, for now there is keen recognition of God's spirit within the person.

An understanding of the nature of empathy yields knowledge of the self — the "I" — as person, but also knowledge of "the other." Knowledge of self is perceived in actual experience, but knowledge of the "other" is gained through empathy. Because I cannot doubt the consciousness of my own experience as given to my "I life," I understand that the "other I" also has thoughts, emotions, and sensations. I understand the consciousness of the other through empathy.

In the next chapter, "The Person in Society," we shall pursue empathy in relation to "the other" as the basis of social consciousness. Let us first concentrate on Edith Stein's philosophy of the physical-psychical-spiritual person per se. She asks what the term "person" signifies and finds two levels of meaning. Primarily, personhood rests on the "pure I" which is independent of time and place. The second level of meaning lies in the flood of consciousness involving personal experience, which has both time and place and marks our individuality.

The soul carries the personal stream of consciousness, its attributes, habits, and attitudes. It is the center of reference for sensations, emotions and volitions. And its special unity stems from the particular content of its own stream of experience. The soul is the habitat of the "I life" which wills and controls "the lived-body." Edith describes this "lived-body" as a unity of localized sensations, and these feelings, in great part, constitute the nature of consciousness.

We express our feelings through acts. But because we are spiritual creatures, we need motivation to propel our feelings into act. We seek a meaning content in our acts; thus, motivation is the law preceding action. The person goes from one act to another in a meaning context. Indeed, the physical-psychical person becomes the spiritual person as the one who acts, for action proceeds "meaningfully from the total structure of the person" (*Empathy*, 112).

Although the action of the will is free and autonomous, it is not always able to overcome the limitations of the physical-psychical being; yet the will can master both body and soul. But the will is also based on feelings. The thought "I want" is affirmed by "I can" and then "I will." This element of action is determinate of the spiritual person as distinct from the physical-psychical person. The spiritual person is aware of feelings and levels of meaning and is motivated into action. And these voluntary acts born of spirit shape not only personal but social and cultural life.

For we enter here into the spiritual world of values which transcends the natural world. Again, it is the emotional life which opens the world of values because they are understood through feelings. And, Edith Stein writes, one cannot understand the person without knowing his/her doctrine of values.

We have spoken of meaning as the basis of motivation which rules action. And, indeed, writes Edith Stein, there is a meaning of life itself found in the particular unfolding of each person, for there is in each person "an unchangeable kernel, the personal structure" (*Empathy*, 110). There could be a defective unfolding or no unfolding at all. A person can be an incomplete person, one who cannot love or hate, appreciate nature and art, or experience values. Such a person is a phantom for he does not experience a selfhood. Yet a spiritual person can exist even if unfolded in this sense.

Let us pursue this unfolding of personhood as given in the later work of Edith Stein. We will meet an exciting development of these major themes which I have so briefly presented here. Now, as a Christian philosopher, she adds great wealth of mind and spirit in her analysis of the person.

The Later Phase — Christian Philosophy

Each one of us is created — designed by God — to be His image and likeness. In fact, we *are* His image. But since the nature of fallen humanity renders us far less than perfect, God gave us His resplendent image, Christ, to lead us back to perfect nature.

We have noted before that, according to Edith Stein, the final goal of education is the attainment of original nature given by God. Education thus plays an important role in the process of shaping the human personality: it supplies formative materials constantly integrated by the physical-psychical person. The end result is the *gestalt* — the shape of the soul. But other factors enter in. The person is responsible for self-formation, but it is God who is the Master Educator. And He is forming what He Himself has given us. She writes: "Just as *an inner form resides* in the seed of plants, an invisible force making a fir tree shoot up here and a beech there, there is in this way an inner mold set in human beings which urges the evolution into a certain direction and works towards a certain *gestalt* in blind singleness of purpose, that of the personality which is mature, fully developed and uniquely human" (*Essays*, 130).

Can we not also say that the seed planted within each person for a "fully developed and uniquely human" personality is actually the image of God, which God has Himself instilled in each of us and who watches and guards its growth to fruition? In the fullness of the redeemed order, each person will reflect God's image purely and totally. For, Edith Stein writes, the fullness of personhood can be found only in God; all faculties are developed only in knowing, loving, and serving Him.

The Divine Being is the archetype of all finite personal being (*EES*, 323). The individual person is most like divine Being in the very fact that he / she is a person, because God is personal Being. Thus the primary *Analogia Entis* implies "the relation of the divine 'I am' to the multiplicity of finite being." Every man is an "I." We as created persons are a "part image" of God, but Christ is God's perfect image for He and God are one (*EES*, 321).

Edith writes that only a person can create. The rational order and aim of the world indicate its creator as a personal agent, because "reason and freedom are essential marks of the Person." She quotes St. Augustine who writes that the primary basis of our likeness to the divine *is* in thought: "The person is an hypostasy among whose attributes is dignity; and because it is a great dignity to be the carrier of a rationally-endowed nature, each individual creature of a rationally-endowed nature is called person" (*EES*, 330).

She ventures further: if person is a reason-endowed nature, then person also expresses a spiritual nature because spirit and reason are inseparable. Hence, spirituality and personhood are connected. The "I" inherent in the person is understood as personal life freely fashioning itself.

Let us discuss this last concept more fully. We have seen that, in her earlier work, Edith has defined person as physical-psychical-spiritual. Now as a Christian philosopher, she adds depths of meaning. She offers the analysis of her friend Hedwig Conrad-Martius concerning the constitution of the person: corporeal being is an earthly entity which is "born out" of itself and unfolds its shape, manifesting what it is inclusively. Soul is the "hidden life" from which the physical entity attains embodiment and which urges the embodiment's unfolding as a becoming entity. Spirit is "supra-worldly," able to leave self in devotion to others; it is a "fixed unfolding" of perfect selflessness (*EES*, 229-30).

The words "becoming entity" are important here. For Edith tells us, in line with Aristotle and the Scholastics, that living creatures are distinct from inanimate objects in that there is a shaping power within (the soul) which changes matter (the lived-body). In this being and becoming, there is an intended unfolding. The being "becomes," "develops," "unfolds" to the perfection of its nature as a full self.

She writes that God leads each person in his/her own path. Some come more easily and quickly to the goal than others. What we can do personally is actually little compared to what is done in us, but we have to do that little. Above all, this means to pray persistently for the right path and to follow the call of grace when it becomes evident, without any resistance. Only one may not set a time limit for the Lord! (Neyer, 23).

"Thus our being is revealed to us as a continual becoming and passing away and always only approaching true being. The idea of true being is that which is perfect and eternally changeless — pure act." By pure act, Edith of course means God, while humanity is in the constant flux of potency and act. "My present being is actual and potential being, real and possible at the same time...." And, following Aquinas, she writes, "What a man *does* is the realization of what he *can* and what he can is the expression of what he *is*; his essence comes to the highest development of being in his ability to realize himself through his doing" (*EES*, 38-47).

Our inner awareness of this personal experience is the "I life" and this life is built by the stream of new experiences. According to Husserl, it is the "pure I" which lives in every "I perceive," "I think," "I draw conclusions," "I rejoice," and "I wish"; it is also the I which focuses on its own thoughts, perceptions and wishes. All this consideration of the "I life" is the life of the soul, which as we have seen, is the nature of a lived-body.

But this nature has meaning and authority, inasmuch as the soul is ordered through its particular nature to a determined end and that it is empowered to become what it should be. "The power unfolds in the life of the soul" (*EES*, 399). "Life is a temporal, moment to moment progressing" (*EES*, 458) …a receiving, for the personal I is given life in two ways — in consciousness of self and freedom to fashion itself.

We have spoken of the *Analogia Entis* as the likeness of creation to God. This relation of temporal to eternal Being explains the human drive for a full unfolding from potential to real Being, which God is. There is a power within urging the human being to progress to an excellence of being: efficacy is that power which propels a personality's dynamic unfolding to reach full actuality. This "excellence of being" awakens the spiritual life in the inner core of the soul: the heart, mind, and will. For this, the "I" learns to dwell in its interior depths, to be self-contained, to possess itself in its drive to "real being." Here the "I" feels the meaning and power of its life and attains its fullness.

The interior life so described is the true center of physical-psychical-spiritual being. A person's nature radiates from the soul's interior and magnetizes others. "The more recollectedly a man lives in the interior of his soul, the stronger will be the radiation that emanates from him and exercises its spell on others" (*EES*, 405; Graef, *Scholar*, 160). To live in one's interior depths is to harness one's powers, measure little things in the view of eternity, and regulate behavior accordingly. Such a soul is on its way to final formation and to the perfection of its being. Unfortunately, Edith writes, most people live on the periphery of their being. And, she adds in a footnote, "Our Holy

Mother Teresa says that it is surely an ambiguous, indeed, ab-normal condition that one does not know his own house" (*EES*, 395, fn. 877).

A great part of our material here is taken from her defini-tive philosophical work *Endliches und Ewiges Sein*. Let us also refer to her final study, *The Science of the Cross*, where she of-fers a wonderful account of free spiritual behavior which re-sides in the soul's interior. This is found in a section composed of Edith Stein's own philosophy rather than the general con-tent concerning St. John of the Cross. This section is entitled "The Soul in the Realm of Spirit and the Spirits."

Edith writes that the person is created to live in her/his inmost being. Here the soul possesses and rules itself by way of its ego, which is most free in the deepest part of the soul's interior. Only from this depth can a person make free decisions, relate to others, and find his/her allotted place in the world. "If a man is not wholly master of himself, he will not be able to dispose of anything with true freedom, but will be subject to external influences" (*Science*, 119).

We have said that Edith writes, "reason and freedom are essential marks of the person" (*EES*, 317). It is the free person who understands his condition, looks for and is aware of mean-ing, and decisively acts. We have seen that the term "motiva-tion" defines the spiritual meaning which sets the soul into motion. The person should examine his/her attitude respon-sibly and intelligently, take a stand, and freely act.

But the highest act of personal freedom is surrender to God. And God helps the soul to surrender freely to Him in or-der to bring it to union with Him. It is in the interior depth that union with God takes place. But God also respects the soul's freedom to surrender because He wants to be Lord of the soul through its free gift of love. Surely Edith is voicing an old Ger-man prayer: "God take me from myself and give myself totally to you." Detachment from self is of great importance to avoid anguish and anxiety. This surrender leads to perfection of self, and not only to personal union with God but serves to lead others to that same union. Here Edith is following St. Teresa of Avila who taught "we become true persons only when we find God deep inside of ourselves."

Thus the soul's life in its interior depths offers the experience of the indwelling of God in the soul. God directs every soul, but grace is only possible when freely accepted. This divine life is triune: the love of Father and Son breathing the Holy Spirit. Here Edith carries the concept of the *Analogia Entis* still further: the human person resembles the divine Godhead who is Three Persons.

She asks: "If the Creator is the archetype of creation, then should we not find in creation a likeness insofar as it is also the three-in-oneness of primary being?" (*EES*, 328). She answers, "There is thus in the entire scope of real entities a three-way unfolding of being" (*EES*, 334).

"There is a united three-way unfolding of the body, soul, and spiritual life. These image the Father, Son, and Holy Spirit. God the Father is linked to psychical being; the soul images our Prime Creator by creating in a flow of divine life out of itself and by providing the source of life. God the Son, begotten not made, is seen as living nature: Christ is the 'inner word' within the person, forming the shape of the lived-body in His image. God the Holy Spirit is seen as the free and selfless flow of spirit which moves within us in gratuitous acts, renewing the face of the earth from its 'streams of living waters'; for the Holy Spirit knows, in the divine light within, the first intended shape of creation, despite the 'deformed husks' it has become" (*EES*, 425-26).

But "what does spirit mean?" Edith asks. It is entirely selfless because it gives itself up completely in contrast to the aloneness of the psyche. She writes,

In the complete self-giving of the divine persons, in which each completely divests his nature and still perfectly preserves it, each wholly in itself and in the others, we have the spirit in its purest and most complete realization for us. The triune Godhead *is* the proper "kingdom of the spirit": — simply the "heavenly." All spirituality or spirit-endowment of creatures signifies an "elevation" to this kingdom though in different senses and in different ways (*EES*, 333).

A person is united to God in the inter-Trinitarian life in his/her interior life. This affects personal action. Edith writes that a person relives the Trinitarian life of mutual surrender when giving self totally to God for love of neighbor, in imitation of Christ crucified. Indeed, such human love is triune in nature: "...the perfection of one's own being, union with God, and work for the union of others with God and of the perfection of their being are all inseparably united" (*Science*, 216).

To do this, one must have full empathy with Christ, i.e., "enter into the mind of our Lord on the cross" (Ibid). One cannot help but wonder if the young Jewess Edith, sitting in the class of Max Scheler, heard him speak the following words. This wonderful passage is from Scheler's essay "The Saint, the Genius, and the Hero."

I ask the question: what is it that the saints who "followed Christ" wanted, experienced or did.... They wanted to *co-live* and *re-live* in one act the Spirit of his (Christ's) historically fortuitous, small and poor life. And this they did, of course, along quite different contents of their lives, in terms of quite different experiences, deeds, actions, and works. Yet, they leavened and saturated all their fortuitous qualities, talents, milieus, historical situations, occupations and duties, with the individual essence of Christ's person. This amounts to a unique jump into the center of a person; it amounts to an intuitively seizing hold of its well, and a "life" from out of this center, i.e., every one of them living his own, fortuitous, historical life.... It is this "center" that his followers had of him, possessed, and acted out in such lived manner which is holy and alone can be called so. They thusly eternalize the being and life of his person through actions everlasting insofar as they re-live and co-live them. The original holy man, in contrast to a genius living on through his works, possesses "presence of self." This self-presence consists in the *coincidence* of his being, works and actions, in the nature of his personality. And for this reason the "presence" of the original saint who is "person" through and through, is neither dependent upon, nor conditioned by, the destiny of any one of his works which are different from his very being. He "himself" can truly be present without being restricted by any material symbols. And since the material with which the original saint works and creates is neither wood, stone, nor paint but the person of the human being itself and, therefore, of all possible human beings, he can only be present through and in *persons.* In persons, however, he can *in truth* be present (Scheler, *Person*, 161-62).

Of course, this passage suggests how Scheler influenced Edith Stein. But it is much more than that. It explains not only the presence of Christ in Edith, but describes her holiness and impact on other persons. And Edith was concerned with how the person attains holiness. We have come full circle. Christ is the perfect image of God, Edith writes. But we are also destined to be the image of God, for He planted the seed of this image of Himself within each person. This creates human solidarity, for we are all united in the Mystical Body of Christ with Christ as the Head of humanity.

We are each called to become "another Christ," for He is the perfect gestalt — the shape — of the soul, "the archetype of all personality and the embodiment of all value" (*Essays*, 259). He is "the concrete image of total humanity." In imitation of Christ, the person thus becomes fully human. This is not only to image God, but in accordance with true humanity, it is to become one's true self.

We have witnessed a journey of spirit. When the dark ego is surrendered to God in perfect freedom, when the spirit desires only God's will and relates all actions to Him, the person has matured to a wholeness of spirit. This *is* actually holiness and attainment of the image of God as Person.

Is the Embryo a Person?

In her writings, Edith Stein does not argue the question of abortion directly. But we do find specific answers to the problem in her concepts on the nature of the woman, person, embryo, family, community, humanity, existence, and the Indwelling of God in the human soul.

We have said that the person images God the Creator in providing the source of life. God is linked to psychical being, and this gives witness to the psychical union of man and woman. This union was the first community, "a community of love," she writes. The child is a gift from God and receives its unique psychic stamp at the inception of life.

We have just answered the question, "When does a fetus become a person?" Edith also writes that Mary's Immaculate Conception reveals the presence of spirit in the embryo at the very beginning of its conception. "If the most Blessed Virgin Mary could be free of the stain of earthly sin at the moment of her conception, then at this moment is the union of the soul with the lived-body and the beginning of the transfer of existence" (*EES*, 472).

And Edith likens the mother's free acceptance of her pregnancy to Mary's "Yes" to the Incarnation. Just as Mary was the gateway of the Redeemer, so each woman who welcomes motherhood performs an act of grace. Like Mary, a woman is to "devote the entire kingdom of her soul to the soul of her child" (*EES*, 473).

In pregnancy, a woman's entire being is united and given over, physically and spiritually, to the formation of a new person within. In doing so, her own personhood is enhanced. We have seen that a woman's mission is to defend and nourish life. Her soul is meant to shelter within itself the unfolding soul of another person. How true this must be for the new soul enclosed within her own bodily shelter. And so close is this union of mother and child that to harm the embryo is to harm herself.

Because of its psychic receptivity, the embryo receives spiritual as well as physical nourishment and formation from the mother. Edith voices a conviction upheld by modern medicine: "The child's soul receives impressions from what he sees, hears, and touches; indeed, even experiences before birth can leave impressions upon the soul, and these impressions can have unpredictable consequences in later life" (*Essays*, 242).

She offers an example of the inner life and receptivity for impressions present in the embryo: John the Baptist leaps for joy in the womb of Elizabeth when she meets Mary. What an amazingly beautiful argument this is for the presence of a person in the embryo and the sacredness of life from its very beginning!

And then, the "motherliness," the "spiritual maternity,"

which Edith Stein views as the essence of woman, totally be-
lies the validity of abortion. She has said that woman's ministering love is an attribute of God's Spirit poured out over His
creation, that her most specific and exalted vocation as a woman
is to vicariously help others to their perfection. In this love, we
can see the selfless flow of the Holy Spirit moving to renew the
face of the earth.

And Christ? We have said that He is "the inner word"
forming the shape of the soul in His image. In different ways,
Edith likens human birth to that of the Incarnation. Just as God
needed Mary for Christ's birth, so is the woman needed to
impregnate life and grace into new persons, new members of
Christ's body, the Church.

She offers a beautiful metaphor regarding human birth,
the Incarnation, and the spiritual expectancy during Advent.
In a letter written just before Christmas 1934 from the Cologne
Carmel, we find: "Surely you often visit our choir in spirit now,
because you know how well one can spend a silent Advent
here, *as secure as an unborn child waiting for the great day of new
birth*" (*S-P*, 192). This analogy linking the mystery of Christ's
birth to His birth within a person spiritually, and to human
physical birth, testifies to the value and sanctity of human life.

Thus the image of God in the person begins in the embryo.
And the unique nature of personhood present there is needed
in God's plan for us. All creation is needed in this plan concerning the Mystical Body of Christ. Each unique personhood
is a part of the wholeness of humanity, which, Edith writes, *is*
the Mystical Body of Christ (*EES*, 478-82). We may ask, will the
abortionist have to answer to God for interfering in His Divine
Economy?

We shall see next that, according to Edith Stein, our personal concern for "the other" as an image of God lays the foundation for a healthy and just society. For our common human
nature expresses in solidarity the natural law upon which hu-

man rights are based. The full development of each person constitutes the common good, but selfishness destroys social harmony. Surely all this speaks against legalized abortion.

She writes that respect for the value of each person constitutes the character of the state, and its power is justified only by supporting human rights. The state loses its foundation if it creates anti-values. Thus, the agents of government are holders of a sacred trust; if it acts contrary to the citizen's religious feelings, a person has the right to act contrary to law.

No, she is not advocating anarchy! But these feisty words are indicative of Edith's objective, balanced, and brilliant views of "The Person in Society," which we will investigate next.

CHAPTER 6

The Person in Society

I. The Free and Conscious Person

We last spoke of Edith Stein's philosophy of the person. "We understand by person the conscious and free 'I'" (*EES*, 347), called to live the interior life: only thus is it possible to face the world. And, she writes, this holy objectivity quickens the soul: "Such a soul reacts to all events in the proper way and at the right depth" (*Science*, 2). Aware of feelings and levels of meaning, the spiritual person is motivated into action, shaping not only his/her personal life but social and cultural life as well.

So the person has to be prepared inwardly to be of fruitful service to others. The voice of conscience is heard in the soul's center, the place of self-giving, free decision, and union with God. From this interior depth, according to one's particular personality, we are called both as individuals and members of the community. And only those who have awakened to this inner life as persons are capable of carrying communal responsibility. Only free and loving spirits can be the servants of God.

II. The Role of Empathy

Edith Stein has told us that the basis of social relationship is empathy between the "I" and "the other." She asks, "How can one throw a bridge from the 'I' to another person?" To answer this question, she also asks, "What is the structure of a person who can, through empathy, approach another person?"

Her colleague, Roman Ingarden, attributes the benefit of her doctoral study, *On the Problem of Empathy*, to her description of the five elements of the person: "the pure I," consciousness, body, soul, and spirit. And, he writes of her analysis: "...all elements build a united whole" although they are not all as clarified as he would wish (Ingarden, 79-80).

Thus, Edith Stein describes the constitution of the human being in order to present a right theory of empathy and true knowledge of the other. We have seen that she views "the question of empathy as the perceiving of foreign subjects and their experience" (*Empathy*, 1). She concludes that we cannot have the other's original experience in its exact sameness, but we do come very close to that by substituting ourselves for that person in his/her experience. Disagreeing with a basic concept given by other philosophers, she writes that she is never *one* with the other and never able to become so; but what one knows of one's own structure as person initiates knowledge of the other.

"We see ourselves spiritually in images of our own nature: we see another in ourself and these images confront us in another man." But not only do we gain knowledge of the other based on the commonality of the human spirit, we also gain in knowledge of self. She quotes Friedrich Schiller: "Do you want to know yourself? Then see what moves another" (*EES*, 322).

Thus, every comprehension of another person enlarges our own personhood. Recognition of the other as a fellow-human being implies respect for him/her. This consciousness of the other as belonging to the same Being — God — is like knowing that one's hand is part of one's own body. Her reverence stems from the Jewish concept of the person as a unique image of God and it embraces those of every religion, culture, and race. This is in keeping with the biblical account of the children of the earth created as one family. This is human solidarity. In our diversity, we human beings have a common significance in our very likeness to God.

Christ's death on the cross is the unifying factor of humanity: as Redeemer and Head of the Mystical Body, Christ's intention was the solidarity of all persons and of humanity with God. Thus we recognize that the Judaeo-Christian tradition steers us to a world of brotherhood and sisterhood, of peace and respect for our neighbor.

She asks, "Who is our neighbor?" Her answer: "Whoever is near us and needing us most is our 'neighbor': it does not matter whether he is related to us or not, whether we like him or not, whether he is morally worthy of our help or not. The love of Christ knows no limits" (Graef, *Writings*, 25-26).

Let us compare this to the beautiful words of Franz Rosenzweig, the famous Jewish philosopher; this passage is found in *The Star of Redemption*:

> ...man is to love his neighbor like himself. Like himself. Your neighbor is "like thee," "like you," and thus not you. You remain You and you are to remain just that. But he is not to remain a He for you, and thus a mere it for your You. Rather he is like You, like your You, a You like You, an I — a soul (Rosenzweig, 239-40).

III. The Individual and the Community

Edith writes that, in order to recognize a common humanity, and to know oneself as an integral, responsible part of it,
one must be advanced in personal development. With the first
awakening of reason, one is part of an intimate community like
the family or other formative group. There has not yet been any
opportunity to observe larger groups, as an entire tribe, folk,
race, or total humanity. But these smaller communities do provide the necessary paths to experience total human reality. For
we understand the hidden oneness in the intimate community.
Identification with one's own community is important since we
contrast this to others with whom we may be acquainted and
whom we judge as behaving strangely, as being foreign to us.

Yet, this experience of the human oneness in our own community prepares us for the comprehension of humanity as an
encompassing and basic whole. In spite of all differences, we
find ourselves united with people of all times and places. We
are enriched and replenished through our contact with persons
who are conditioned differently.

Could it have been the state of international hostilities
during World War I which inspired Edith to write about the
harmony possible in authentic communal life? Of course, she
had already based her focus on empathy as basic to cultural
sciences and the human community. We are told by those who
knew her that the thought of community was important to her
in her personal life, not just in theory (Ingarden, 57). We do
know that she worked on a treatise, *The Individual and the Community*, which was completed just before the Armistice in 1919.

Edith tells us here that the shared experience of spiritual
persons constitutes community, for empathy is its core. She
views community as a living organism composed of spiritual
persons. The living connection between two persons is *vitalized*
through a spiritual meaning mutually received and experi-

enced. We have seen that emotions and attitudes give access to the world of values. Common motivation regarding these values creates community: the same attitude, understanding, consideration of action, and common behavior. This common experience results from the same spiritual functions (*Beiträge*, 162, 168).

Therefore, the living, vitalized connection between two persons is basic to community. This vital energy *is* its vital force, and its strength depends on the spiritual strength of persons devoted to this social body. Solidarity can reign in such a living community.

The spiritual grace of persons constitutes the "we" concept which moves into action. Communication and law follow. And consciousness of the "we" also makes possible the spirit of a people or of a race (*Beiträge*, 118-26). But, Edith Stein always insists, basic to this communal structure is mutual respect. In the language of Martin Buber, she writes, the relationship between persons must be "I-you" — not "I-him" (just as we have witnessed in the words of Rosenzweig).

This personal relationship must be enriched by contact with other spiritual persons. But society-at-large lacks this real living contact. It is made of varying interests and motives, not mutual interests. Rather than possessing the vibrant, living relationship between the individual and the community, society is a mechanistic, rational milieu without a soul. For that reason an honest society is not possible. And its framework of industrialization works against interpersonal relations. Thus, individuals are alienated and life in common is undermined.

IV. An Investigation on the State

For Edith Stein, the state is like a community, a living organism composed of spiritual persons. Both state and communal life entail an "us" awareness. But only spiritual persons can have personal relationships for the state itself has no soul. It is the communal bonding of persons within the state that certifies its existence; hence, an existing community is the basis of a concrete state. Thus, she investigates the communal life of the members of the state in order to determine the structure of the state.

Her study entitled "An Investigation on the State" was written during the early 1920's, still her intense time as a phenomenologist. She was motivated by her natural political bent, identification with the existential person, and the ferment of the times. Hitler's ideology was being loudly proclaimed as he became leader of the National Socialist German Workers Party in 1921. His manifesto, *Mein Kampf*, was published in 1924 and 1926. Her study was printed in 1925.

In this work, Edith examines the whole gamut of national life: its psychological, philosophical, political, and spiritual elements. It remains a phenomenological study as she describes the state's essence and structure. Its first section is entitled "The Ontological Structure of the State." Here she examines the nation as a community under government control, human rights, natural factors which influence state structure and citizenry, questions of freedom and sovereignty, and the question of people and nation. The second division, entitled "The State Under the Aspect of Values," considers the state and justice, moral values, state and church, etc.

She asks questions most pertinent today in face of the millions of refugees seeking asylum. We are only too familiar with the problems of immigration and the resulting hostility to the foreigner — xenophobia — caused by the dismantling of countries, ethnic purging, racism, etc. In voicing her considerations, Edith seems almost prophetic for us today.

Can individuals live in a state without bonding to each other? We have already answered this question: the state depends on communal life based on the relationships of spiritual persons. The state is the middle type of community: the most intimate is that which is wholly inclusive, such as family and friendship. The very opposite type is that all-embracing community of spiritual individuals.

Then she asks: Does a state consist of one homogenous ethnic group? Or can it embrace in itself a majority of independent and demarcated units of peoples? Her answer is a sobering one in face of the international turmoil we witness today: the community under state control need not be a national community. What, then, constitutes a national community, i.e., a nation? It is an existing stream of life shared consciously by its vocal majority. Each individual carries the stamp of communal affiliation in a continued solidarity. Those persons cut off from national life should be restored by personal contact with its members.

Does the state need a national community as its foundation? In theory, no, since loyal citizens could relate to the state regarding rights and duties. But this could be a very tenuous basis for government since the hostile attitude of its members could cause desire for its overthrow.

Then, she asks: What is the possibility of a combination of nations in one state? We cannot help but think of the dismantling of Yugoslavia and its aftermath. She answers that this possibility exists if each nation is loyal and its uniqueness maintained. But if conflict exists between the nationalities and their loyalty to the state, one or both could go down. However, she writes, this is also possible in a uniform nation where one people is privileged over another.

One wonders, is she here thinking of the Jewish people reduced to sub-citizen status by Nazi ideology and eventually disposed of as "sub-humans" along with other ethnic and national communities?

Edith writes that the real foundation needed by the state

is provided by its peoples, in enough numbers to guarantee its independence from other states and sovereignty over its citizens. It is people who create the national culture, for this is only possible on the foundation of folklore. The term "nation" refers to the unique culture created by spiritual unity, national personality, and susceptibility to its world of values. This can endure even when sovereignty fades (as we saw in Poland and other countries under the Communist regime).

As in all wars, the end of World War I witnessed the relocation of national boundaries. Edith asks a pertinent question: Does a national community subsist only within certain geographical boundaries? She answers that the tie of territory need not be constitutive of the people. This has been witnessed with nomads and colonial possessions. A national community (a nation) needs three elements: the link between continuing generations, the particular type recognizable as a national member, and, most important, the creation of a national culture by its people. Thus, a unity of land and of people is unconnected. Even a spiritual realm can be the basis of a national community.

But, she writes, the natural factors of a geographical territory are related to its inhabitants, their characters and activities. The gloom or charm of a landscape can inspire or defeat. In fact, the land's character can create the personal type of race formed by the influence of natural factors. When the race type becomes a cultural personality, a people is developed. Territory is also a factor through its climate and the nature of soil. The various geographical bodies differ in size and social formations, the smallest being the tribe. And then, our entire economic structure depends on the characteristics of an area.

But, she writes, the particular spirit of the people can compensate for the lack of natural resources. Is Edith here combating Hitler's brutal call for *"Lebensraum"* — living space? She maintains that man's activity changes the life of a state; it is not determined by natural factors alone. It is the spirit that creates the national culture, and the area receives its political meaning through positive communal activities, not territorial limits.

Edith Stein has thus examined the possible forms of coexistence of the subjects within a state in an investigation of its living, its ontological, structure. She has examined it as a governed community of the persons living within it. It is only natural that her inquiry leads her to a consideration of the rights of the state and of its citizens. This forms the second part of the first section in this work on the state. First, what are human rights? In a footnote, she acknowledges that she is indebted here to the work of Adolf Reinach, her beloved teacher of Göttingen University who had died in the war.

V. Human Rights, Natural Law, and Justice

She identifies "pure right" as that human right due to all persons throughout time and place: this is based on natural law and inscribed eternally in the human heart. Whereas positive right is manifested in time and place, created arbitrarily or through political power.

She writes, natural law and the social contract are the basis of the modern state and modern life. The state deals with the valid rights of citizens according to their natural rights. It fosters the free development of persons through the passage of positive rights and injunctions ordering right behavior. And, "wherever pure right is in power, there is justice."

We have come upon a subject dear to all of us and, I am sure, to Edith Stein: human rights, the natural law, and justice. Her self-offering written on Palm Sunday in 1939 was directed to the overthrow of Hitler and the establishment of peace. Belief in the moral values adhering to the human person was a great part of Edith's own cosmic vision and moral courage, which ultimately led her to Auschwitz.

On the question of natural law, she is close to Thomas Aquinas who, in the *Summa Theologica,* defines it as "the participation in the eternal law by rational creatures." "...This ... rational knowledge... is based on our perception of natural goals or inclinations 'that are naturally apprehended by reason as good'" (Kretzmann, 223).

But the social contract exists for the common good. Edith Stein writes that we do not have a problem recognizing our own needs and wishes — but those of our neighbor? We have seen that the concept of empathy is basic to all her works — political, philosophical and spiritual. It is also a theme of her poetry. In a poem *"Der Nächste" (Our Neighbor)*, we find an impassioned protest versus the bigotry of humankind. She writes,

> We cannot separate love for God from love for man.
> We acknowledge God easily, but our brother?
> Those with whom we do not identify in his
>   background, education, race, complexion.
> We could not have imagined that love for God
>   could be so hard. (Herbstrith, *Beten*, 23)

Yet all of us have God's natural law stamped on our hearts. And, "...every creature has its own meaning, and that is its particular way of being an image of the divine being" *(Essays,* 196). "For the Christian there is no stranger" (Graef, *Writings*, 25), words of Edith Stein so antithetical to the contemporary dislike of the stranger existing everywhere. I believe Edith Stein would have suffered very badly had she witnessed today's world. Her thrust was for community, communication and reconciliation — not rejection, hostility, and violence. Christ's intention became hers: solidarity with all humanity in God. His was her love for all.

She states plainly in her study on empathy that we are conditioned by others to dislike persons different from ourselves. The tenor of her political writings, as well as her nature of compassionate love, leads us to believe that she would be audible today in defense of immigration. This, of course, is a worldwide problem, not just America's. Writing today she might pose another question: Do foreigners seeking asylum from war and terror, poverty, starvation, and, finally, genocide itself, do these wretched of the earth have the *human right* to be granted asylum by another country? I think her answer would have been an emphatic "Yes," just as that voiced by Pope John XXIII in *Pacem in Terris*. He writes that exiles are persons whose human rights must be recognized: they do not lose their rights because they are no longer citizens of a different state; in fact, it is the duty of a state to welcome them and allow them to make a better life (John XXIII, 34-38).

We remember, we are to put ourselves into the shoes of the other in order to understand him/her as person. Edith's own pilgrimage led her to put herself not only into the shoes of the oppressed but, in the very shoes of Christ, to walk in His footsteps to the end. As a young philosopher, she writes in *Empathy* that to play proxy is to substitute oneself for the other in consciousness in order to gain the needed understanding. In her later works as a Christian philosopher, contemplative and mystic, she offers the concept of *"Stellvertretung"*, i.e., playing proxy as the means of mediation through prayer for the other's spiritual welfare. Christ, of course, is the supreme mediator and we share in His redemptive action through this intercessory prayer. "The path of human destiny is a path from Christ to Christ" (Herbstrith, *Beten,* 25).

In her poem "Jesus of Nazareth," Edith writes of Christ as a human being in a very personal way. She finds in Him an ever deeper and deeper humanity and love. She compares Him to the Nazis' way of rhetoric, propaganda and violence, and we easily recognize their hatred for "the other" as compared to Christ's love. She asks, "Christ, who suffers for me in this world? Who died for me freely out of love?" (Herbstrith, *Beten*, 27). "No one else but Jesus," she answers, "the Crucified and Resurrected." So ardent is her tone that one experiences the source of her strength in her imitation of His suffering and immolation (Herbstrith, *Beten*, 27).

Her concept of personal action, taken through the medium of intercessory prayer, is extended to embrace the entire family of humanity. This element of personal responsibility becomes then a communal one: the individual person prays for all and all are to pray for the one, for the sins of another become our responsibility in prayer. Seen in this light, our concern for all others' welfare is of a political as well as religious nature: mediation for others becomes a necessary human act, for to help restore the integrity of humankind is to hasten a world of justice. Thus a deep religious meaning penetrates conditions of injustice. This is the spiritual world of solidarity.

Edith Stein has written that the person can perfect self fully only in the service of God; for the highest development of personality comes only by developing one's spiritual powers. Certainly, love for one's fellow creatures is here a vital point.

God is the source of all human rights. The spirit within the person directs the will to right action, and for this we need God's grace. Only spiritual persons can uphold moral values, hence these must be considered as personal values. The state is not a moral being; it does not know, feel, or judge where its duty lies. Only persons can lead the state to act rightly and to translate urgent needs into positive law.

In her talks of 1932 and 1933, Edith Stein spoke out fiercely against Nazi ideology. These years witnessed the sunset of the Weimar Republic and the rise of National Socialism. She voiced protest against the "*Weltanschauung*" (vision of the world) which seeks "to consider all individuals as similar atoms in a mechanistically ordered structure. Such a society and educational system consider humanity and the relationship of the sexes merely on a biological basis, fail to realize the special significance and the higher level of the spiritual as compared to the physical, and, above all are lacking completely in any supernatural orientation" (*Essays*, 206). Rather, she writes, it is the obligation of the state to develop each person's capacities for the perfection of his/her personhood. It helps to do this by granting full human rights.

She stresses the need for all persons to take responsibility for their political and social scene, the need to fight for moral integrity and human values — for the individual, the family, the community and the nation. She warned that Germans must strive hard to keep the democracy, to unite with Europe to ward off the evil inclinations coming in with National Socialism. She urged women to struggle along with men for world peace on an international level.

Here is another question in her study on the state written in the 1920's: How can we reconcile the sovereignty of the state and the freedom of its citizens? She writes that the state is sovereign only by the free consent of its members, while the citizens are free by the state's protection of human rights. To institute rights and to institute itself, the state must make use of free persons; it cannot strip them of their freedom.

In Edith's time of a budding totalitarianism, already present in Italy and emerging in Germany, she upholds democracy as the best form of state government; but she also writes that democracy lends itself more easily than any other form to corruption. She supports the uprising of citizens against an unjust regime, for a sovereign state is justified only by ensuring the rights and freedom of its citizens. She warns that unlimited power can exist only when recognized; at any time it can be struck down.

Justice therefore depends on the strength of persons to exercise it within the state as well as in the state's relations to other states. And, she stresses, there cannot be international peace unless there is justice within each nation.

She suggests that the state practice prudence towards the church; it should not shackle religious values or obligate their citizens to act against their conscience. If state power causes personal decisions of negative value, then it itself is negative. Should the citizen deny a state's injunction on the basis of faith, there is no doubt that he becomes the enemy of the state by assailing its existence. However, she writes, "Should a responsible person conclude that this is a matter of corruption of religious feeling, we can concede that he has the right to act without regard for upholding the law" (Stein, *Beiträge*, 406).

We are now in the second part of her study, "The State Under the Aspect of Values." She discusses the dichotomy between church and state, writing, "There is no real solution to this conflict." But the scriptural admonition to "render to God what is God's and to Caesar what is Caesar's" can be the basis of a smooth co-existence of church and state (*Beiträge*, 402).

Moral values are personal values which reflect personal attitude and lifestyle. This differs from *ethical norms* which are abstractions like pure rights. Only the moral person can lead the state to act rightly by transforming the citizens' moral needs into positive rights. We return always to the spiritual person who acts for the rights of "the other." Viewed in this way, every political, social, and economic action intended for the common good is a spiritual act and God is there to grant the grace for the right action. "And behind all things of value to be found in the world stands the *person of the Creator* who, as prefigurement, encloses all earthly values in Himself and transcends them" (*Essays*, 256).

Justice has been defined as: "rendering to each one his/her due." It is motivated and empowered by love, and "love of neighbor and justice cannot be separated" (La Farge, 88). This is the essence of Edith Stein's focus.

She believes that the quality of justice is formed and developed existentially, i.e., through education and right example. She differentiates this taught quality from those inherited by the individual, such as goodness, purity, and nobility. For the individual develops under impressions from around him. "Under other circumstances, he would have developed differently." Even the "virtuous man" educated in "moral principles" can become corrupt under circumstances of life or environmental influences (*Empathy*, 10-11).

VI. Conclusion

We have said that only free persons can enact justice. Edith Stein raises here a fundamental question concerning human freedom, one that divides modern society. Where do rights and freedom co-exist and where do they part company? Are certain rights claimed today in fact human rights or rather self-indulgences mistakenly claimed as freedom? Edith Stein tells us that true freedom comes only through union with God and adherence to His law. There is no need to elaborate on the dearth of moral values today. Our great loss is in the disorders existing in human personalities which in turn create a disordered society.

Edith tells us that God's original creation was one of pure order and harmony between nature, humanity, and God. For the restoration of original order, each person is to be fulfilled as person in harmony with self, others and God, functioning in his/her place in the Mystical Body of Christ. For Christ came to re-establish the original, harmonious order. He is head of humanity, calling us to perfect peace within, which is harmony in accordance with His way, His truth, and His life.

She writes that men and women together were given the mandate to know the world and take proper charge of it, to enjoy it, and creatively to make it a better world. Each generation contributes to this evolution, and the quality of a given time depends on each person. All of us are related through time and place, for humanity is one family in the process of growth. The end, one hopes, is an assemblage of all persons into the Mystical Body of Christ. Rather than national and international conflicts, there will be an eternal harmony among men: the Kingdom of God.

Let us then do as St. Benedict instructs, and as our Blessed Edith Stein does: "We must run, and do all that will have worth (value) for eternity" (Posselt, 53).

PART THREE

Ecumenism and Edith Stein

CHAPTER 7

A Beatification and Its Problems

For those of us who are followers of Christ, there is no doubt that Edith Stein is a gift from God. She faithfully reveals God's sanctity for it is in her. She also reveals a fullness of humanity perfected in love. But we know that this perfection comes through a crucifixion of self and a resurrection through Christ.

Edith Stein believed in the possibility of universal brotherhood. But those who strive for peace and justice have to carry the cross of Christ. It seems as if every great person in history has been martyred, and, so too, was Edith Stein.

This the Christians believe. But how does the Jewish community respond to this convert who, they believe, abandoned their sacred faith and is being eulogized and honored by the Catholic Church for doing so?

At the end of January, 1987, the media announced that Edith Stein had been declared "Venerable" by the Vatican, a martyr of the Church, and possessor of heroic virtues in fidelity to the gospels. Declaration of her martyrdom meant that a miracle would not be required for her oncoming beatification.

This announcement was the fruit of a process of almost twenty years. In 1958, the Prioress of the Cologne Carmel and author of the first biography on Edith, Sister Teresa Posselt of the Holy Spirit, received the request of the Master General of the Carmelite order to assemble all records and writings of Edith Stein; these were to be directed to the Congregation for the Causes of Saints. She performed this sacred work until her death in 1961, and it was finished by the Vice Postulator of Edith's cause, Dr. Jakob Schlafke. In 1962, Joseph Cardinal Frings opened the Beatification Process and heard testimony from all relevant witnesses. In 1972, Joseph Cardinal Höffner of Cologne sent this file to Rome. Proof of her heroic virtue was established as well as her sanctity in life, death, and after-death, a sanctity worthy of imitation and intercession.

In the fall of 1987, the Jewish community reacted to the announcement of her expected beatification with excitement and pain. The outraged community asked, "Why honor her? Why single her out from all the millions who had died in the Holocaust?" Of course, the fact of her conversion was a real stumbling block in the Jewish-Catholic dialogue because it raises questions which go to the heart of the Jewish-Christian relationship.

Many Jews feared that through her beatification, the Church was trying to legitimize a militant conversion of Jews. Forced conversion had been their plague down through the centuries. The Second Vatican Council document, *Nostra Aetate* (Declaration on the Relationship of the Church to Non-Christian Religions), had seemed to discourage the trend to proselytize Jews. Was the Church now reversing its position? (See Polish, "Painful Legacy," 153-55.)

We must remember that the Jews had come to accept the Shoah as part of their sacred history, as "sancta." It was an historic intrusion of God like the Exodus, Babylonian exile, and destruction of the two temples. Was the Church now seeking to appropriate the Shoah as its own? After all, it was already guilty of supercession: it had assumed the term Israel to mean the New Church, the new People of God; it had taken over the scripture and liturgy from the Chosen People and made them its own. This appropriation of the "sancta" of another faith expresses to the Jews a seeming triumph of the Church over their faith; this raises the charge of triumphalism.

And was the Church trying to say that attention to the victims of the Holocaust should only be paid to those who were Catholic converts? Edith Stein was not only a convert: it was said that she prayed for the conversion of the Jews and had offered her life as atonement for their disbelief in Christ. How could she be declared a martyr by the Church when she had died simply because she had been born Jewish as had all six million Jews? Most awful of all, was the Church trying to divert the world from their own guilt in having remained silent throughout the Holocaust, a silence which for many amounted to complicity with the Nazi brutality?

Just about the time her beatification was announced, shock in the Jewish community was deepened by two other factors: the interview which Pope John Paul II granted to the Austrian prime minister Kurt Waldheim who was known as a former Nazi; and the announced intention to establish a Carmel near the site of Auschwitz, partly in memory of Edith Stein.

The presence of the nuns at Auschwitz again meant to the Jews that the Church was trying to take over Jewish salvific history and the particularity of the Jewish experience. For them, the site was not to be viewed as a place of universal sin and redemption, because the majority of those who had died at Auschwitz were Jews. They realize that the concept of the cross is born of the Jewish experience of redemption and salvation; yet they are horrified by the Christian response to the Holocaust in terms of the cross, and this includes Edith Stein's intention. For them, the cross brings only images of Jewish martyrdom through the centuries of crusades and pogroms. There were even fears that the nuns in the Auschwitz Carmel were praying for their conversion.

The Auschwitz Carmel raised a furious controversy in the media, strained relationships between Jewish and Catholic communities, and became the worst crisis ever in modern times between Jews and Poles. After much deliberation, the Carmel was finally moved a distance from the camp.

It seemed to the Jews that all this was a continuation of historical anti-Semitism. One rightly asks, what are the causes of anti-Semitism? Of course, we are only too familiar with the charge of fratricide and deicide, charges now flatly condemned and forbidden by the Church. Father Edward Flannery tells us of other reasons in his fine study, *The Anguish of the Jews*. Because Judaism declares itself a "chosen people," they are suspected of considering themselves to be better than others. Because of their love for God and His moral laws, they are hated not only by pagans but by a secular society selfishly engrossed in materialism and pleasure. Because many Jews become financially successful through their excellence of intellect and talent, they become a scapegoat for social and economic ills. Jacques Maritain remarks that we should rather transform our social and economic structure instead of using Jews as scapegoats. Although their rate of assimilation is now over 50%, they have always feared it. Because of this need for survival, they have previously kept to themselves; thus in many countries, they have looked and acted differently, thus inciting that suspicion and hostility for "the other."

The Nazis claimed that a deeper chasm lay between those they declared "sub-humans" (Jews, gypsies, homosexuals, etc.) and their Aryan elite than there exists between the highest form of animal life and the lowest human form. This denigration of their humanity caused great moral pain, perhaps worse than suffering from the horrendous physical conditions to which they were subjected. And then, many Jews felt abandoned by God as well as by the world, so silent did He seem to their misery.

This feeling of abandonment was not only for themselves as individual persons. For many it seemed to be God's abandonment of His chosen ones. Their sacred history was recalled, times when the anger of God rose against Israel for its infidelity. After He had brought them into the beautiful land of Israel, they proved unfaithful and incurred His wrath, thus prompting the psalmist to sing: "He gave his people to the sword, in his anger against his chosen ones" (Psalm 78). As the early psalmist, so did the Nazi prisoners now cry out to God against their oppressors: "It is for you we face death all day long / and are counted as sheep for the slaughter" (Psalm 44).

Since the Shoah, a remarkable healing has taken place which allows many Jews to accept the Shoah as part of their "sanctum." But this healing made all the more reprehensible what they consider to be a denial by the Catholic Church of the Jewish role as primary victim of the Holocaust.

How differently the Church views the honoring of its faithful servant of heroic virtue: Edith Stein or Sister Teresa Benedicta of the Cross. They raise her up not as a convert but as an ideal human being to be emulated by the faithful. The intention has been one of reconciliation with the Jewish community, not the inflicting of further pain upon it. In honoring her, it wishes to honor as well all the millions of victims martyred by the Holocaust.

A statement was issued in April, 1987 — just after the announcement of the beatification — by the Secretariat for Catholic-Jewish Relations of the National Council of Catholic Bishops. It reads in part:

> Catholic respect for the integrity of Judaism and for the ongoing validity of God's irrevocable covenant with the Jewish people is solidly founded on our faith in the unshakable faithfulness of God's own word. Therefore, in no way can the beatification of Edith

Stein be understood by Catholics as giving impetus to unwarranted proselytizing among the Jewish community. On the contrary, it urges us to ponder the continuing religious significance of Jewish traditions, with which we have so much in common, and to approach Jews not as potential "objects" of conversion but rather as bearers of a unique witness to the Name of the One God of Israel (Fisher, 25).

In the case of the Auschwitz Carmel, it was stressed that no inordinate motivation was present. Rather the intention was in accordance with traditional Carmelite spirituality of expiation enacted through silence and prayer. In regard to neither the beatification nor the Carmel was there any intention but reverence, certainly not that of subsuming the Shoah by the Church.

We have said that the cross distresses many Jews because many of the Nazis were baptized Christians. They even believe that many of the Nazis were practicing Christians. But we know that in Europe the term "Christian" had more political and racial connotations than religious. Robert Martin tells us, "While it was true that in 1939 the vast majority of people in Europe (excluding the Soviet Union) were baptized Christians and eight out of 10 of these were Catholic, only a small minority were regular churchgoers" (Martin, 1).

Ambrose Eszer, a German Dominican who acted as Relator for Edith Stein's cause for beatification, writes that the Nazis were "an example of the consequences of a massive collapse of Christian ethics over vast segments of the population of entire nations, in particular the Austro-Germanic population" (Eszer, 318-19). In his study on the martyr status of Edith, he writes that it was a hatred for the faith (*odium fidei*) which led to the killing of the baptized Jews in Holland along with the Jewish community.

Exceptions had been made from deportation for baptized Catholics by the Reichscommissar, Dr. Arthur Seyss-Inquart. However, this was changed on July 26, 1942, when a pastoral letter was read from every Dutch pulpit protesting the deportation of the Jews; they also protested the Nazi exclusion of the children of Catholic converts from Catholic schools — the only means left for their education. The Protestant Churches had at first intended to participate in this protest with the Catholics under the directive of Bishop de Jong, the Archbishop of Utrecht. But the Nazis had heard of the intended action on July 26th; they sent warning to the Churches not to carry it out, promising that the authorities would not deport Jews who were baptized before January of 1941.

Some of the Evangelical Churches held fast but most refrained from the protest. The Catholics not only read the Pastoral Letter but also the Nazi telegram warning them not to do so.

On the following Sunday, August 2nd, all Jews who had been baptized Catholics were arrested, Edith and her sister Rosa among them. Some Jewish Protestants were picked up but later returned. There is no doubt but that the roundup was a retaliatory measure made in hatred of the Church. The very next day, a notice was placed in the newspaper by the Commissar which reported that the National Socialists realized that Jewish Catholics were the worst enemies of the Reich and had to get them out of Holland to the East as soon as possible (Kawa, 83).

It is sad that the true character of Edith Stein's prayer was lost in this confusion, for the Jewish community has identified her with political implications attributed to the Church. We have already spoken much of her intentions and self-offering. It is said that she prayed for the conversion of the Jews and perhaps she did, but there is no available written evidence to that effect. However, there is a recorded document of two

Dutch men, sent by the Echt Carmel, who visited her in Camp Westerbork just before she was sent to Auschwitz. She told them that she wanted to offer up her suffering for the conversion of atheists, for all who no longer love God, for her suffering fellow Jews, and for the Nazi persecutors (Herbstrith, *Edith Stein* [Ignatius, 1992], 185).

The opening of the beatification controversy in the press can be traced to the Jewish writer James Baade; yet he wrote, "However, she proposed her sacrifice for the sake of 'true peace' in the world, not the conversion of the Jews" (See Baade).

Preceding the beatification, there was much said in the Jewish community about the phrase "disbelief of the Jews" attributed to her will of 1939. The wording, however, is clear. She is directing prayer to "der Herr" — God — and not to Christ, which would have been "der Herr Jesu"; and Edith Stein always said exactly what she meant. As we have noted, she offered up her life and death for the glory of God, for world peace, the intentions of the Church, Jesus, and Mary, the religious Orders — especially the Carmelite, the deliverance of Germany and her relatives, and she prays for the Jews — that they will turn from disbelief to belief *in God.*

Edith Stein was undoubtedly sensitive to the existing Jewish agnosticism of her time which included members of her own family. She herself had not received "a strictly orthodox upbringing." Two of her Courant cousins actually went to a convent school for a year. Her sister Elsa had a non-religious wedding because she and her husband were non-believers. This is the family where she spent ten months during what she calls her atheistic period. Remembrance of this time must have made the whole question of Jewish agnosticism difficult for her; she recalled painfully the condition of her own soul before her conversion as due to "sins of radical disbelief." She writes that the Jewish agnostics, mostly middle-class intellectuals, felt superior to the Protestants in both background and station. In fact, they were so assimilated that they did not believe the Nazi threats since they considered themselves as German as Hitler was. Perhaps she thought also of the later years when her grown siblings tried to discourage her mother from following all the Jewish prescriptions (*Life*, 160, 180, 128, 169).

She always maintained great reverence for the faith of her mother and her people. Written evidence contradicts the substance of the rumors concerning her intentions. After the death of Edmund Husserl, who had for many years not practiced the Christian faith, she writes to her dear friend Sr. Adelgundis Jaegerschmid who had nursed Husserl at the end.

> I am not at all worried about my dear Master. It has always been far from me to think that God's mercy allows itself to be circumscribed by the visible Church's boundaries. God is truth. All who seek truth seek God, whether this is clear to them or not (*S-P*, 272).

Edith writes that the Carmelite stands before all for God because Christ died for all. The head and body of one Christ constitutes the unity of the human race. "It seems to me to belong to the meaning of the Mystical Body of Christ that there are no men — outside of sin — who do not belong to the unity of life of this body" (see the closing pages of *EES*). Each person is designed to be a member through redeeming grace and to share the Redeemer's life.

We are told that any thought of proselytizing among her Jewish friends would have been embarrassing to her. The philosopher Gertrud Koebner, a Jewish friend of Edith, stresses that Edith Stein was ecumenical long before Vatican II.

The truth is that because Edith was holy, she wanted everybody else to be holy in their own faith. She was interested in the conversion of heart that brings a person to God. And she felt deeply the needs of the Jewish community because she considered herself still a member of that community. In their view, Edith had cut herself off by her conversion. But in her that could never be, for her Jewishness was the very soil where Christianity took root in her. And she reacted with anguish at every expression of anti-Semitism.

The blessed day of Edith Stein's beatification finally arrived. It was May 1, 1987. Your author was one of the honorary guests of Joseph Cardinal Höffner, Archbishop of Cologne. I sat with her family and friends directly in front of the altar. Five of her nephews and nieces came with their families ranging in age from 25 to 85 years. They had travelled from the United States, South America and various countries in Europe. Former students from Speyer and Münster were there.

Seventy thousand people were assembled in the Müngersdorfer Stadium in Cologne. Many persons without a ticket stood on the streets outside, proudly bearing her picture in solidarity with this historic event. Yes, there was some disturbance on the outside created by dissenters. But the day wore a radiance all its own. Cardinal Höffner's words of greeting in the Mass booklet confirmed what each participant felt: he noted that in this beatification, one sees the unity of 887 million Catholics worldwide.

Our Holy Father arrived in his "Popemobile" and circled the stadium to the delight of the people. In the cape he wore for the Mass were sewn parts of Edith's bridal dress worn at her investiture on April 15, 1934. There were fifteen concelebrants: eight cardinals, five bishops and archbishops, and two priests.

John Paul II declared Sister Teresa Benedicta of the Cross "as blessed in the glory of God. From this moment on we can honor her as a martyr and ask for her intercession at the throne of God." He expressed special joy in the presence of the Carmelite Order and her relatives (John Paul II, *L'Osservatore Romano*, #20, p. 19).

In the Penitential Rite, the lector read this heartfelt act of contrition:

> Sin and guilt lie over humanity. The shadow of im-
> measurable sin and guilt weighs on the history of our
> German people. We are called to atone for the past
> and to answer today for peace and justice through a
> new way of thought and a deeply engaged concern.

Cardinal Höffner formally presented the request to pub-
licly honor Edith Stein in the name of the faithful. The Holy
Father answered by declaring the Heroic Servant of God be so
named in the future as Blessed, and the day of her death, August 9th, be understood as her feastday.

In acknowledgment of Edith's prayer of intercession for
her people in terms of the biblical Queen Esther, the reading
was taken from the book of Esther. It ended with the words,
"Save us with your hand. Help me for I am alone and have no
one other than you, O Lord" (*Eucharistiefeier*, 17).

The gospel reading was from John 4:19 describing the
meeting of Christ with the Samaritan woman. Jesus says, "Salvation comes from the Jews." Then the Holy Father delivered
his homily. How beautiful he was himself that day as he spoke
his words of love: love for her, the Church, the Jewish community, and all humanity. His deep love for Edith Stein was ap-
parent in the tone of his voice and his holy understanding of
her spirituality and meaning. Calling her a faithful daughter
of both Israel and the Church, he conveyed her as a symbol of
the Jewish-Christian tradition and the reconciliation possible
between all faiths; also, she is a symbol of the persecuted and
oppressed of all times, certainly a symbol of the millions who
had died during the Holocaust. Many times his words seemed
to echo the sentiments and thoughts of Edith. He included as
the oppressed those in the third world crying from their mis-

ery, a call which every person is responsible to heed. He said truthfully that the whole world was her church.

Some of her family present were Protestants, most were Jewish. There have been negative reports regarding those of Edith's family who attended the beatification ceremony. However, I know many of them personally, sat with them during the event, attended with them the special reception which followed the ceremony, and I do not believe that their attitude can be described as hostile. In one case perhaps yes, and perhaps some ambivalence, but otherwise there was also appreciation and wonder, especially from the Protestant branch of the family.

But unforgettable was the absolute delight and radiance of her Carmelite sisters. At times during the Mass, nuns among others who were her good friends spoke of her modesty, humility and goodness. But this was certainly a wonderfully joyous event for each person in the stadium. They had come from every continent on the earth. Why had they come? It seemed for all a unique confirmation of their own faith. The beatification was demonstrating their own faith as alive and active, functioning in the intention of Christ's teaching in a perfect and balanced order. The deepest intentions of one's spiritual being were here open in full recognition and realization.

In the offertory, one felt that each soul was surrendering fully in prayer and intention. Part of the procession was the presentation of earth from the original site of the Cologne Carmel where Edith had lived, as well as earth from Camp Westerbork where she was interned a few days before her death journey to Auchwitz. Also part of the offertory gifts were her own works, and writings about her.

As the Mass progressed, excerpts from her own recorded prayers and writings were read. The communion was efficiently distributed by the eucharistic ministers in all parts of the stadium. The people remained in their places as communion was brought to them.

John Paul II now told us that Edith is blessed in the holiness of God and calls each one of us ever deeper into the mystery of God's redemption. He prayed in her name that we might today overcome injustice in the entire world, that this day's benediction will lead us in a blessing that will heal rifts that exist between all peoples and faiths.

As if in answer to his words and final blessing, the stadium became aglow with light, real and spiritual light, as runners entered swiftly, each bearing a torch — the Altenberger Light. They had come, as they do each year from the Cathedral of Altenberg, carrying a symbol of reconciliation and peace.

There remain many questions to be answered for both faiths, Jewish and Catholic, in order for final reconciliation to take place. Through both scripture and liturgy, the Church proclaims that the cross is the only path of salvation for the world. Jesus himself said, "I am the way and the truth and the life. No one comes to the Father except through me" (John 14:6). Edith Stein understood the destiny of the Jewish people as under the cross and therefore wished to take it upon herself in the name of all. And yet I have written of her,

> She anticipated the ecumenical concerns of today. Her belief that no one is exempt from salvation by the outer limits of a particular church preceded the declarations of the Second Vatican Council. She lives the reality of the continuing validity of Judaism in its own right and as the heritage of Christianity (Oben, "Edith Stein in Light," 32).

Her views were confirmed by the Second Vatican Council in its "Declaration on the Relationship of the Church to Non-Christian Religions" (*Nostra Aetate*). One of her fervent admirers was Msgr. John Oesterreicher, a Jewish convert. In 1960, he led a group in petition to the Vatican that a statement regarding Jews be included in the coming agenda. He wrote the first draft of the section on the Jews and led its revision for the final document. It was certainly in Edith's spirit that he addressed the following words to a wavering Council: "The Church awaits that day known to God alone, on which all peoples will address the Lord in a single voice and serve Him with one accord..." (Oesterreicher, 231).

What does this statement regarding the Jews say in Part Four of *Nostra Aetate*?

The human race is to be a single community whose one final goal is God. The Church acknowledges the "sacred link," the "spiritual bond," between Judaism and Christianity and the revelation which we receive from Hebrew Scripture. Jews remain dear to God who does not forget his promises to them. The charge of deicide — that Jews are collectively guilty of Christ's death — is repudiated as well as anti-Semitism of all times and places. In fact, any deprivation of the human rights of others because of race, color, life condition or faith precludes the Catholic from union with God.

Christ died for the sins of all so that He might win salvation for all. Thus, the Church is acknowledging that salvation is there for everyone without sin. Yet, it proclaims the cross as "the fountain from which every grace flows." Also, Christ is "the way, the truth, and the life in whom men find the fullness of the religious life and in whom God has reconciled all things to Himself" (Abbott, 664-68).

We find other answers in another Vatican Council document, the "Dogmatic Constitution on Divine Revelation" (Abbott, 111-122). "Natural revelation" designates the fact that all created reality manifests God. He fully revealed Himself to Adam and Eve and, after the Fall, watched over humanity "in order to give eternal life to those who perseveringly do good in search of salvation." God called Abraham to father the great Jewish nation; they were taught to revere God and await the

Messiah through Moses, the prophets and patriarchs.

A valuable in-depth discussion of revelation and salvation can be found in the text *The Diversity of Religions* by the Dominican friar Augustine DiNoia, theological consultant for the National Council of Catholic Bishops. He refers to "general revelation" as God's "presumably widespread dispersion of true and wholesome teachings in other religious communities.... The unique valuation of the Christian community and of its particular role in divine providence does not preclude the attribution to other communities of some role in God's plan for the salvation of the world."

The relations between the Jewish and Christian faiths affect the Christian formulations of all faiths. The providential role of the Jewish community in history, only dimly perceived now, should be more thoroughly examined and defined by the Church. Karl Rahner is among other theologians who believe that Judaism and other religions offer valuable doctrines from which Christians can learn. Father DiNoia uses the following terms to describe two different views: "inclusiveness" which considers other faith doctrines as supportive of Christian values, thus possibly leading to the acceptance of the Christian faith; and "pluralism" which views doctrines depicting aims other than those of one or all communities (DiNoia, 86-94).

Indeed, belief in the diversity of religious aims as part of God's providence is in keeping with the Christian concept of universal salvation. Another document of Vatican II, "The Dogmatic Constitution on the Church" (*Lumen Gentium*), states plainly that "the plan of salvation also includes those who acknowledge the Creator." Included are those who do not know Christ but who strive to do God's will as they understand it in conscience. Thus, Jews and Moslems and others who seek God and acknowledge Him are included in His salvific plan. Included also are those who do not know God but live a good life in His grace.

Does all this not sound just like Edith Stein? So, to the question, "Can non-Christians attain salvation?," the answer is a resounding "Yes!" The beliefs, values and way of life of non-Christian religions afford a plan of salvation which does not have to coincide with Christianity. Yet, the Church considers that the goodness or truth of other life philosophies is preparation for the Gospel (See Abbott, 14-101). "...all human beings who have ever lived... are called to participate in a relationship of union with the Triune God" (DiNoia, 70-73).

Another disturbing rift between our two faith communities has been Jewish apprehension concerning the role of the Church during the Holocaust. Except for those called "righteous Gentiles," this role is viewed negatively. Long awaited, a document titled "We Remember: A Reflection on the Shoah" was issued in 1998 by the Vatican Commission for Religious Relations With the Jews.

Its Preface is a letter from our Holy Father, who stresses the need to repent all past errors and to assume responsibility for the evils of our time. "The forgiveness of sins and reconciliation with God and neighbor" is required for a joyful celebration of Christianity's third millennium.

The statement names and deplores two wrongful attitudes: anti-Semitism denies "the equal dignity of all races and people" as evidenced in National Socialism; anti-Judaism is "the long-standing sentiment of mistrust and hostility" evidenced through history. Both kinds of hostility must not be allowed to root or to grow further. The Church regrets all past anti-Semitism and invites all its members to remember that the roots of Christianity lie in Judaism. They are to think on the Shoah and resolve that it will never happen again. Indeed, the Church repudiates the persecution of every people, everywhere.

One sentence holds connotations of Edith Stein: "This is an act of repentance (*teshuva*) since as members of the Church, we are linked to the sins as well as the merits of all her children" (Cassidy, 13). Thus the Church is clearly expressing sorrow and repentance for the failure of Catholics to better resist the evil of the Shoah. However, some prominent Jewish figures have voiced disappointment in the document for denying that National Socialism was rooted in historic Church anti-Semitism and encouraged by anti-Semitic Christians of the time.

It does acknowledge that many Christians failed to act as Christians not just during the Holocaust but in every age. It lauds those persons who did resist, especially Pope Pius XII whom many Jews view negatively.

Yet it was to be hoped that this vital statement from the Church, spoken in terms of sorrow and repentance, would help to dispel tensions with their elder brothers, and that one day, indeed, the world will cry out to God in one voice.

CHAPTER 8

St. Teresa Benedicta of the Cross, Edith Stein

Story of a Miracle

L'Osservatore Romano had announced that the canonization for Edith Stein would take place on October 11th of that year, 1998. The American media, however, was slow to convey this news. In May the Vatican approval of the necessary miracle for the coming canonization was made known everywhere.

Only two miracles are needed now for canonization instead of the four required before 1983. Should the candidate be declared a martyr, as in the case of Edith Stein, only one miracle is needed. Edith's cause for beatification had been approved on January 26, 1987; during the following March, the needed miracle occurred. Its subject was a two-year-old named in Edith's honor, Teresia Benedicta McCarthy, the child of Mary and Rev. Emmanuel Charles McCarthy, a Catholic priest of the Eastern rite.

The couple had left their twelve children to go to a retreat in Rome. When they returned on Friday, March 20th, they were told that the baby had been hospitalized. "Benedicta was lethargic, delirious and vomiting." At first it was believed that she had spinal meningitis, but then many wrappings of extra strength Tylenol samples were found; she had taken sixteen times the toxic dose.

It was believed that she was dying. There was infection. She needed a liver transplant and her kidneys were failing. She was moved from the local hospital to the Massachusetts General Hospital in Boston. Her main physician, Dr. Ronald Kleinman, did not expect her to recover. Even if she got a transplant, there was only a fifty percent chance for survival, and she would still have to be on medicine for the rest of her life.

Teresia's father, Rev. McCarthy, was a co-founder of Pax Christi USA dedicated to non-violence. He had begun an annual practice of fasting for forty days, ending on August 9th: his intention, that Christian consciousness would be enlightened, for August 9th is the anniversary of the American bombing of Nagasaki which for him epitomizes the callous violence of which Christians are capable. He soon learned that this is also the date of Edith Stein's death. His daughter Teresia was born on August 8th, 1984 but it was August 9th in Polish time — Auschwitz time. We can say that August 9th held great significance for Father McCarthy!

He was committed to go that Sunday, March 22 to lead a retreat in Minnesota until Tuesday. But how could he go? He remembered the words of Teresa of Avila: "You take care of my business, and I'll take care of your business." And so he went.

Mrs. McCarthy and her family decided to pray to Edith Stein for Teresia's recovery, and they called about asking others to share in their intention. Hands were placed over Teresia in the area of the liver as they asked for Edith to intercede. On Monday, there was hesitation regarding the necessity of a liver transplant. Tuesday afternoon, the chart read, "This child has made a remarkable recovery." And by the end of the week, she was released as completely healed. No prescription would be needed for further medication.

A few weeks later, on May 1st, Edith was beatified. The McCarthys decided to go public with what they believed was a miracle. Dr. Kleinman, a Jew, concurred: "I was willing to say that it was miraculous that she turned around." Dr. James McDonough, former president of the Massachusetts Medical Society and member of the American panel which examined her cause, said, "What convinced me was the rapidity with which she got better."

The material presented to you here on the miracle is a compilation of testimony given by Father McCarthy and by the Carmelite scholar Kieran Kavanaugh, who gave invaluable service as the Vice Postulator of Edith Stein's cause. The investigation was "very, very careful, very deliberate," said Dr. Kleinman. "I didn't at any point feel that this was a foregone conclusion" (Keeler, 30). In fact, there were serious difficulties. Some doctors were of the opinion that her recovery was natural and that no transplant had been needed. Dr. Kleinman was given more credence as the major attending physician. He explained that the required procedure of administering an antidote, which could induce a natural recovery from toxicity, had been delayed and given too late to allow for a normal recovery, or, in fact, for the rapid recovery which had taken place in just 24 hours after Edith's intercession was invoked.

The American records were turned over to Rome. Again, there were difficulties. Dr. Kleinman went to Rome and conferred with a team of five Italian doctors. In January, this team concurred with Dr. Kleinman that Teresia's recovery from "multi-organ failure" was indeed extraordinary. In April, the Bishops agreed, and in May, the world received the announcement of the approved miracle.

We Are Present at the Canonization of Edith Stein

Edith Stein writes that Jesus Christ is the ultimate truth. Now in Rome, on the day of her canonization, it is as if the entire Church were greeting and acknowledging her in the wonder of this truth. Tens and tens of thousands slowly fill St. Peter's square, jubilant and blessed. A solidarity of spirit reigns, as if each soul were praying, "Make us holy, O Lord, for this day has come." The presence of the Religious does not predominate over that of the secular. Edith is a peoples' saint, confirming their faith by her absolute faith, trust, and enactment of Christ's gospel.

October 11, 1998 is a warm and golden-lit day. The gaze of all who enter the square is immediately drawn to the huge banner mounted high above the great portals of St. Peter's Church: it depicts the soon to be declared saint in her religious habit. Under this banner, and adjacent to the church door, is a platform serving as a sanctuary, which is slowly being filled by dignitaries from Church and state, and other special guests as they arrive. The guests are seated on both sides and behind the altar.

Teresia Benedicta McCarthy, the "miracle" child now become a teenager, is present with her parents — Rev. Emmanuel McCarthy and his wife Mary. Ninety-seven members of the Stein family, spanning three generations, are here.

The political dignitaries include outgoing German Chancellor Helmut Krol and the Polish Prime Minister Jerzy Busek, from whose countries have come many parishes, all carrying banners announcing their locality. The German contingent alone is estimated at twenty thousand. But pilgrims have come from all over the world: cardinals, bishops, and pastors from France, America, and, of course, from Italy. The major cities where Edith lived, taught, and lectured are well represented, such as by Henryk Roman Gulbinowicz, Archbishop of Wroclaw, formerly Breslau — the city in which Edith was born;

Archbishop Joachim Meisner from Cologne — where Edith first entered Carmel in 1933. But then there are representatives from distant places where Edith had never been, such as Baghdad, Madrid, and sites in Mexico.

Important officials from the various branches of the Vatican are seen: Bernardin Gantin, Dean of the Sacred College of Cardinals; Joseph Ratzinger, Prefect for the Congregation of the Faithful; Vergilio Noe, Archpriest of the Vatican Basilica. Carmelite officials, such as Father Joseph Chalmers, the Prior General of the Carmelite Order, project the special Carmelite jubilance, not to speak of the happy Carmelite nuns present.

Friends greet each other in real delight, while singers and musicians rimming the high balustrade which frames the courtyard reinforce the radiant atmosphere by their marvellous music. The Sistine Chapel Choir sings in Latin and, as the morning progresses, choirs and their orchestras from Cologne and Münster are also heard. And it is a colorful day. The red of the hierarchy is challenged by the even more flamboyant dress of the Pope's Swiss guards: smiles appear on many faces as they look upon these brilliant orange and black uniforms, red plumes and red cuffs, silver helmets and collars, and the white gloved hands clutching large spears. A large crowd of youngsters, some of whom act as minor ministers of the altar, are dressed in red cassocks and white surplices, creating a scene mindful of Easter morning.

The entrance of Pope John Paul II incites a robust cheer from the crowd, as he takes his seat to preside from his chair placed in the center of the sanctuary. Readers give a continuous biography of her life delivered in French, Italian, German, Polish and English. The biographical details highlight Edith as a young Jewess, philosopher, atheist, working woman, and Carmelite; the documentation is taken mostly from her own *Life in a Jewish Family* and *Edith Stein*, her first biography by Sr. Teresa Posselt, who had been her novice mistress in Cologne.

After the "Kyrie, eleison" is chanted, there comes the Introductory Rite of Canonization. First, it is declared that the Church joyfully offers Edith Stein, "daughter of Israel and daughter of Carmel" as witness to the victory over evil through the cross. "The bow of the mighty has been broken/ Life is more powerful than death "(*Canonizzazione*, 111). Then the Prefect of The Congregation for the Causes of Saints, Archbishop José Saraiva Martins, and the Postulator, Father Simeone of the Sacred Family, ask the Holy Father to declare her sainthood. The Litany of the Saints is recited, after which the Pope declares in Latin:

> For the honor of the Blessed Trinity, the exaltation of the Catholic Faith and the fostering of the Christian life, by the authority of our Lord Jesus Christ, of the Holy Apostles Peter and Paul, and our own, after due deliberation and frequent prayers for divine assistance, and having sought the counsel of many of our Brethren in the Episcopate, we declare and define that Blessed Teresa Benedicta of the Cross, Edith Stein, is a Saint and we enroll her among the Saints, decreeing that she is to be venerated in the whole Church as one of the Saints.... Your servant Teresa Benedicta of the Cross, Edith Stein, crowned with glory and honor, graciously intercedes for us from her radiant place in heaven (*Canonizzazione*, 123-25).

After the declaration of sainthood, there is a great burst of applause for St. Teresa Benedicta of the Cross from the estimated 60,000 persons present.

The "Gloria" is sung. This author thinks of a few lines opening an essay by our new Saint: "The Significance of Woman's Intrinsic Value in National Life." Here she describes the praises to the Lord continuously being sung in the Beuron

Abbey from which she had just come: "Day after day, year after year — *a custodia matutina usque ad noctem*" ("a watch from morning until night"). And she adds that now, back in the secular world where she is lecturing, it is "almost like dropping from heaven to earth" (*Essays*, 253). On this day in St. Peter's Square, it seems as if that celestial choir in heaven were listening to the choir in the square as it sings "Glory to God" for her sainthood.

The readings are like those at her Beatification. The first is from the Book of Esther 4:17; this passage calls to mind Edith's analogy: her prayers being offered to God for the safety of the Jews as were those of the Hebrew queen of old. The first stanza of Psalm 18 is the Responsorial Psalm. As it is sung by the choir with exquisite beauty, one cannot help but wonder: Is Edith, such an avid lover of the psalms, also listening? The second reading is from St. Paul's letter to the Galatians 6:14-16: "It is out of the question that I should boast at all, except of the cross of our Lord Jesus Christ." The Gospel, chanted in Latin and in Greek, is again as at the Beatification, John 4:19-24, in which we hear "for salvation comes from the Jews," and then, "true worshippers will worship the Father in Spirit and in Truth" (*Canonizzazione*, 147-149).

Our Holy Father develops themes from these readings in his homily spoken in both Italian and German. Like the apostle, he declares, Edith's sole boast is the cross of Christ, for in the mystery of love, she was given courage and strength to follow in Christ's footsteps. "*A young woman in search of the truth has become a saint and martyr through the silent workings of divine grace.... Let us give glory to God for what he has accomplished in Edith Stein*" (John Paul II, *L'Osservatore*, #41, pp. 1 and 10).

Our Holy Father now extends his greetings to all the diverse groups present, particularly to the members of the Stein family. He reminds us that, when a possible way out was offered to Edith just before the train departed to Auschwitz, she had refused: wishing to share the lot of her Jewish brothers and sisters, she could not accept help unavailable to them as well. But the world will remember the Shoah in all its horror as they celebrate her yearly feast. And, raising his voice in high penetration, he exclaims: "For the love of God and man, once again I raise an anguished cry. *May such criminal deeds never be repeated* against any ethnic group, against any race, in any corner of the world" (Ibid., 10). When he repeats the homily in another language, he again raises his voice at this sentence, and each time the response is equally high in approval.

He continues: in freedom, Edith sought for truth and finally found it in the love of Christ; she realized that "only those who commit themselves to the love of Christ become truly free." And he urges the young people present to pay attention — to put their freedom in God's hands. "St. Teresa Benedicta of the Cross was able to understand that the love of Christ and human freedom are intertwined, because love and truth have an intrinsic relationship.... One without the other becomes a destructive lie" (Ibid.).

So also do love and suffering intertwine: "*Love makes suffering fruitful and suffering deepens love.*" As Edith developed in devotion to the cross, "she found the roots to which the tree of her own life was attached," and understood her unique vocation to live the cross. May she be an example to us to serve freedom in truth. "May her witness constantly strengthen the *bridge of mutual understanding between Jews and Christians*. St. Teresa Benedicta of the Cross, pray for us. Amen." (Ibid.)

The Mass is concelebrated by twenty-six Cardinals, plus many archbishops, bishops, monsignors and priests. One may well wonder how full must be the heart of the Holy Father and all who have labored so hard for her cause, such as Archbishop Franciszek Macharski from Krakow. And then, what must be the joy of the father of the miracle girl, Emmanuel McCarthy, and of the American Vice-Postulator of her cause, Kieran Kavanaugh, who are among the concelebrants!

The Eucharistic prayer declares: "Her death reveals your power shining through our human weakness" (Ibid.). Indeed, at this moment of consecration, one marvels how a mere human being can so authentically follow Christ in His Passion. As the Holy Eucharist is elevated, this pilgrim looks from the raised Host to Edith's face above, and then to the brilliantly lit sky. Suddenly a private truth is realized. When starting to do research on Edith Stein thirty-six years before, I had felt as if I were crawling through a dark tunnel towards a great light. Now, at this moment, I am enveloped in that light, and I pray for holiness, for myself and for all.

The Eucharist is given to the great numbers present, for, by now, over 100,000 persons have gathered. The Angelus is celebrated and the final blessing given. The huge crowd is quickly dispersed by watchful guards who allow no loitering. Many faces are profound, even sad. We have been deeply moved.

The Continuing Controversy

The news coverage of the canonization was disappointing, even humiliating, to the disciples of St. Edith Stein. Rather than focusing on the event's merits, the newspapers were concerned mostly with suggesting its possible negative aspects. The controversy over her beatification was repeated. It was suggested that not only Jews but many Catholics looked askance at the declaration of her sainthood, or at best were lukewarm.

Yet the dissent was not as intense now as at the beatification, and it was on different grounds. There had been a change of perspective in the Jewish community since the beatification a decade before. There had been much inter-faith discussion, not on Edith Stein alone, but especially on the Vatican document issued just months before the canonization, "We Remember: A Reflection on the *Shoah*." This statement of March, 1998 closed with these words: "…the spoiled seeds of anti-Judaism and anti-Semitism must never again be allowed to take root in any human heart" (Cassidy, 14).

Both before and after this vital statement had been issued, important figures from both the Catholic and the Jewish communities were developing lines of fellowship and understanding. There were common efforts from both faiths to together be a "light to the nations": for instance, they joined in an effort to support better family life over the world at the 1994 meeting in Jerusalem, sponsored by the International Catholic-Jewish Liaison Commission. Cardinal Cassidy, as the Vatican Chairman of Religious Relations With the Jews, lit a virtual light of respect when, for the first time at the Vatican, he lit Hanukkah candles.

Scholars had been exchanged between the two faith communities to teach at institutions of higher learning. In fact, programs were set up in high schools as well. Plans were drawn to develop mutual research concerning the Shoah and to disperse this knowledge between both faiths. Healing statements were issued by the various Bishops' Conferences in America and abroad.

Let us not forget the historic visit of Pope John Paul II to the Great Synagogue in Rome in 1986, followed by the establishment of formal relations between Israel and the Vatican, indeed, all the efforts of the beloved Holy Father to make war against anti-Semitism. This has not been unrecognized: he is credited for doing more for the Jewish Community than has occurred in the entire span of Church history. All this had mitigated the climate of Jewish distrust and suspicion toward the Church during the last ten years.

Already in 1991, Rabbi Zev Garber, an American theologian, had said and written, "Jewish fears that the veneration of Sister Teresa would promote conversion among Jews or ap-propriate the Shoah event as a Church tragedy are properly laid to rest in a statement of the Bishops' Committee for Ecumeni-cal and Interreligious Affairs of the National Conference of Catholic Bishops..." (Keeler, 5; Garber, 90). Yet such suspicion remained in a new version: Rabbi Daniel Polish was still able to write at the time of her Canonization, "...a cloud of suspi-cion will always hang over the Church's motive in choosing Edith Stein for canonization" (Polish, in *Never Forget*, 174; he voices the fear that the Church, among other ulterior motives, is trying to "market" souls for the Church through the label "Jewish-Christian").

The controversy continues. On the one hand, there is in great part a withdrawal of charges made against the Church concerning deicide, supercessionism, and "spiritual imperial-ism"; on the other hand, old myths are still repeated concern-ing the new saint's motives towards the Jews, and the attempt of the Church to "universalize" the Holocaust and to look for redemption through Edith's canonization; it would even make easier the placing of crosses on graves adjacent to Auschwitz!

Clearly, there is need for mutual elucidation. Professor Garber raises important issues in need of further discussion: first is the differences in the two faiths on the theology of re-demption.

> For the Church, it is the Easter faith, spirit over mat-ter, that enables victory to be proclaimed over Golgotha and Auschwitz. For the Synagogue, it is the covenantal oath at Sinai, united spirit and matter and resulting in everyday acts of holiness, that permits Zion to triumph over Auschwitz. Recognition of this difference may lessen the Jewish objection to Pope John Paul II's homily in his advocacy for the canoni-zation of a "Jewish" nun (Keeler, 8; Garber, 92-3).

This raises another important question. We do know, certainly, that Edith always continued to feel her Jewishness even after she became a nun. This invites discussion on a long-standing, weighty question, one that has become much more complicated during the twentieth century. Dr. Immanuel Jakobovits, an English Chief Rabbi, opens his work, *Jewish Identity*, with the following:

> For over 3,000 years, whatever arguments and schisms may have divided some Jews from others, they were agreed on the definition of a Jew. He was a person born of a Jewish mother or converted to Judaism according to Jewish law. They asked only, What is a Jew, and in reply to this question they produced a vast literature setting forth the *Orach Chayim*, the "path of life," on which one must walk to be characterized as a Jew. But they never asked, *Who* is a Jew (Jakobovits, 2).

In his writings, the noted historian Raphael Patai has identified Judaism as a race, religion, nation, and lineage (Garber, 79-84). We in modern times have witnessed the tensions between religious and secular Jews, the problems raised within the state of Israel over this question, the frictions caused by assimilation, intermarriage, the differences between the Jews of the diaspora and Israel, and, ultimately, the differences in an understanding of the Shoah which have created severe differences in Jewish theology.

But we are also told that, since the Enlightenment in the nineteenth century, the Jewish community has slowly become diversified in thought and in structure. "Jewry today is divided into a variety of subgroups with their own religious identities": we find the Ultra-Orthodox, Traditionalists, Conservatives, Reconstructionists, the Reform Jews, and agnostics (Cohn-Sherbok, 1-23).

Years ago, Rabbi Jakobovits stated that "The Who is a Jew controversy... lies... at the heart of Jewish peoplehood"; Menachem Begin answered in a Knesset debate that the best definition of a Jew might still be the traditional interpretation of the Jew as one who follows Jewish *Halacha* (Jakobovits, 2 and 5). Now Rabbi Polish notes, the fact that Edith felt like a Jew after her baptism does not make her one: in the Jewish view, one cannot continue to be a Jew while believing in Christ.

The paradox remains. Edith died as a Jewess and as a Christian, in loyalty to her blood and to her faith. Her life was given for the Jews in a pure love, and this she was able to do through her Christian faith. She could do this exquisitely because the Jesus she followed *was* a Jew.

The continuation of Judaism within herself was as alive as is the continuation of Judaism in Christianity. She felt, indeed, the organic sacred link that must always be there. In 1938, Pope Pius XI's voicing of this truth emerged as a little jewel: "Through Christ and in Christ we are of the spiritual lineage of Abraham. Spiritually, we are Semites" (Garber, 84). Edith recognized the Jewish roots of her faith within herself long before it was emphasized in *Nostra Aetate*. The stumbling block, of course, is that for all Christians, Christ is the Messiah promised to the Jews; for Jews, He is not.

St. Edith Stein's faith in Christ was absolute, yet, at the same time, she respected the right of each person to freely pursue his or her own unique spiritual journey. She had been very independent herself: first, as a young Jewess who declared herself an atheist; secondly, by the very act of baptism into Christianity. She could not refuse others the freedom she had exercised in her own search for truth. For her, the excellence of the human person lies in the possession of self in this search for truth which is God.

As a laywoman, her spiritual director was Abbot Raphael Walzer, who said of her that an intention of reconciliation was the pivot of her being. In this ongoing Jewish-Catholic dialogue of differences, surely a keener knowledge of the other will help each faith towards recognition of similarities. "For differences can at times mask deeper commonalities of revealed insight for Judaism and Christianity alike. This is the unending hope of dialogue between us, and the unending goal of reconciliation" (Keeler, 8).

"O Cross, it was from the darkness of your suffering that a new dawn arose" (*Canonizzazione*, 193). May the agony of St. Teresa Benedicta of the Cross yield a new dawn of hope for the two faiths that she so loved.

The Nature of St. Edith Stein's Sainthood

Thus, the discussion found in the news was highly polemic. In the secular press, the nature of her sainthood was ignored. John Paul II has been highly motivated in his frequent, for some too frequent, making of *beati* and saints: our highly disheartened and demoralized times need frequent reminders of the high level of humanity which we mortals are able to attain. The saint is born with God's love for humanity within. St. Edith loved God with the totality of her being: hence she understood God's love in Creation. Indeed, she identified with His creative intention and wanted all in the world to be good and happy.

To various degrees, this is the natural intention of the human heart. Humanity was initially created in harmony but then willfully destroyed its own original perfection: perhaps this is why the human spirit seeks ways to recreate the beauty and the love initially lost. Some persons are born with a lifelong desire to do whatever is possible through their professional work to help return peace to this world. Some persons endeavor to make the world a just and peaceful one by being just and peaceful themselves, by being the best kind of persons in daily life. And then, there are the very few, in every time and place, who do so at the cost of their lives.

Edith knew first hand the beauty and ugliness, the horror and goodness of her own time. At her Beatification, we were told, "Sin and guilt lie over humanity.... Not one of us can say we had nothing to do with it" (*Eucharistiefeier*, 7). And long before the call for repentance in "We Remember," Edith understood and identified with Christ in His intention of reparation to salvage the world from sin and evil. By her witness to God's love in her, she continues now as then, and will in the future, to fight this evil by her sacrifice. We are reminded again of her admonition that good and evil will make war until the end of time as we know it. Thus this saint gladdens our souls with hope that our world can yet be saved.

The term "martyr" means "witness to the faith." Edith Stein was composed and steadfast until death, and she was able to be so in the name of God. The authenticity of her virtues — fortitude, courage, temperance, etc. — all fulfill her title of "Woman of Heroic Virtue" and inspire our own spirituality. She died the death of Christ again, not only spiritually in union with His redemptive action, but physically through her own death. She literally bore His dying in her own flesh. We are reminded of a Christmas reading: "Let our bodies be signs of your life / as we bear your dying in our flesh" (Liturgy I, 623).

She was not born so. She exemplifies par excellence her own philosophy: the person attains perfect "efficacy" by a steadfast pursuit of God. The ordinary person struggles in varying degrees to do this, but we are not all gifted with the strength to withstand the loneliness of the mystic. The saint helps the image of God planted within to reach perfect fruition. In Edith, this came to full maturity as holiness persevered in its way through inner complexities and outer horrors. She won magnificently what she terms the primary vocation of each person: holiness. Sublimating over self and a mundane world, her spirit broke all shackling chains as she attained the perfection of personhood: sainthood.

The Meaning of St. Edith Stein for the Third Millennium

A vital factor is that, in order to find her genius as a Christian philosopher, Edith had to first find the Christian faith. She turned in her search for truth from reason alone to revelation as well. Thus, the bond between her life and her work is found in her faith. This can be seen as one of her vital contributions to the future: she evidences the accord that can exist between science and faith.

The first chapter of her magnum opus *Endliches und Ewiges Sein* is devoted to the question of "The Meaning and Possibility of Christian Philosophy." Here she analyzes and relates reason and revelation, philosophy and theology, science and truth, affirming the Christian philosopher's use of faith as a source of knowledge. She attests that, in the theological use of the word, science is spoken of as a "gift of the holy spirit" (*EES*, 13). And, finally, it is the mystic who wins a "blessed vision": the divine life in which he/she participates grants a share of the divine knowledge (*EES*, 27-28).

Our secular scene needs this greatly. Henri Bergson claimed that "the fluidity of life, the elusive *élan vital* (vital impulse), can, it seems, be known by an examination of those who have plunged into the ocean of life, who have felt the throbbing of the heart of reality, the saints... through them alone can reality be restored, all ethics, all philosophy, all spirituality, all religion" (Calvert, 324).

Edith's creative impulse was tied to her deep inner life. This tie reveals the spiritual essence of reality and lends a sacramental dimension to her words. Like Thomas Aquinas, her genius of spirit is manifested through a brilliant clarity of intellect. Those of us who are not too familiar with philosophy and theology can still be inspired and excited by the content of her work, for her themes go to the heart of human life throughout time and place.

What are good and evil? What is freedom? What is life's meaning? What is the structure of the human person — body, ego, soul, spirit and how do they relate? How can a person best be educated? What is prayer? What is grace? What is being and Being? What is faith? Who is Christ? What is the Trinity? What is death and resurrection? What is communal life? What forms the Church, society, and the world as community? How do we relate to "the other"? How do we communicate? What is the interior life? Edith draws answers from theology as well as philosophy for these and other vital questions.

This work did not come easily to her. She tells us that her intellectual work was a spiritual offering, and that all spiritual work entails the price of suffering. Because our saint loves humanity so much, she wrestled with these questions which we struggle with each day. Some of us, unable to find fulfilling answers, become lost in "modern gloom" or "metaphysical anguish." Many a lost soul could be consoled and strengthened by a knowledge of Edith Stein's life and thought. She urges us on to find divine harmony and order within ourselves, and, in so doing, to find the source of social harmony and order.

Edith writes that we are created with an innate ability to unfold, to progress in our potential spirituality, to take hold of our interior depths in an excellence of being. According to her, we are all beings in the process of becoming, and this also affects the world in *its* becoming. For the quality of humanity depends on the humanity of each person as lived individually. What each "I" is and does determines each generation's collective contribution to humanity and to the unfolding of the world. Thus Edith touches us in our innermost depths, inciting us to an excellence of being, of thought, and of action in our so very muddled world. For once a person is in possession of self in this reach for God, he/she also reaches out to the "other." Maladies of thought and of action cannot survive in the milieu of such excellence of being.

Alfred Delp, martyr of the Holocaust, wrote that "modern man had lost his susceptibility to God" (Oben, *Edith Stein*, 72). Edith challenges contemporary society to rediscover its spiritual life through a life of prayer. By way of her life and work, she gives us in richness the truths that this modern era lacks.

Certainly, she epitomizes her own teaching: the deeper one enters the interior life, the more powerfully is one compelled to bring divine life into the world. She invites us to recognize the solidarity in which we are created, by fostering values and exercising responsibility for each other.

Edith is like an explosion of light in a dark world, a model for the new millennium. She is an example of pure charity in her concern for a just and peaceful world. A successful professional, yet a feminine and spiritual woman, she is a totally integrated person and citizen of the world. She lived the moments of her life consciously and responsibly and calls us to do the same.

Regarding all questions of human existence, she manifests woman's essence of spiritual maternity. This is, of course, seen in her philosophy of the sexes, of youth and the family. Her concepts of the formation of the person through religious education would reduce modern trauma and generally benefit our suffering societies. She stresses that the spiritual formation of youth towards holiness is the primary mission of any given time. Our Holy Father echoes her call as he urges young people all to be saints. By her writings as well as her own example, she encourages women to fulfill their role for the good of humanity. Let us note that she, a woman and yet a highly acclaimed philosopher, was also declared a saint. And the fact that her philosophy of the woman as well as of the person is very important to both the secular world and to the Holy Father, hence to the Church, reveals the magnitude of her contribution.

In this so impersonal world, her work helps us to know ourselves and, thereby, to know God and our neighbor more intimately and more tenderly.

In her, we realize that a particular time needs the particular kind of saint it is given. Perhaps the specific charisma of this saint will be found for many in her dramatic life and death, her intention of reparation, and the hoped for reconciliation between Jews and Christians. For does it not seem that the time for a respectful, understanding Jewish-Christian relationship is now, that the centuries of enmity should be over? Her witness offers hope for the innate goodness of human nature created by God and decries the tragic and criminal abandonment of Jewry by the Christian world. Edith's belief in the providential role of her life has been lived and is being fulfilled. Let us pray to her as guardian of our Jewish-Christian relationship.

Then will the Jewish and Christian communities be effective carriers of justice and moral values. Together, can they not lead to an end of hostilities between one group and all the differing "others"? If they do not advance a combined effort to end all prejudice, who will? Edith writes that the greatest commandment of the prophets and of Christ is to activate the perfecting love of God and neighbor, that in the end all differences will cease and only great love will remain. Quest of such love is the timeless, universal call to each person regardless of a particular race, religion, or nationality, for we all possess the same eternal and universal human nature. We ask: Is not the ecumenical claim deepened by this spiritual solidarity?

It seems that in our exploding technology today, society does become more and more mechanized or, as worded by Edith, "soulless." Yet, traditional Jewish-Christian morality seeks to reverence the person made in the image of God. Is it not plausible that these faith communities should cling together, to also overcome the secular malaise and fanatic forces of today? This is possible, for the most sacred human need is to search for truth: God and His mandates. Edith Stein herself took that arduous trip from atheism to absolute faith. She can help us here.

She overcame the philosophical doubts of her time through the absolute conviction that we are all sustained in being. She declared that nothing is *accidental*, that there is perfect meaning in God's pre-designed providence for each person. And we know that Edith was sustained by God in her sacrifice. Let us not forget her deep reverence and devotion for the Eucharist and for the Crucified Christ. She writes frequently that we cannot overcome the difficulties of the time on our own; but through the sign of the Cross we can overcome all things — personal and cosmic.

In her rare and precious journey, St. Edith Stein bears witness to Christ and so deepens His life in our midst. For Christ touches us and helps us grow through our knowledge of and love for her. Do we not find meaning in the truths she offers each of us in our own existence and journey? And even in our particular salvific journey, we see an ultimate solidarity: we are all one. "The fullness of the divine life can be realized in us only successively, the many members have to complement each other" (Graef, *Writings*, 44).

The saints have great eschatological import: they bring us ever closer to the Kingdom of God.

Bibliography of Works Cited

The author offers here only the works actually cited. It would be impossible to list all the many works consulted during her forty years of research on Edith Stein.

Abbott, Walter M., SJ, Ed. *The Documents of Vatican II.* Very Rev. Msgr. Joseph Gallagher, Trans. New York: America Press, 1966.

Baade, James. "Witness to the Cross" in London's *The Tablet* (April 14, 1984).

Baseheart, Mary Catherine, SCN. "The Encounter of Husserl's Phenomenology and the Philosophy of St. Thomas in Selected Writings of Edith Stein." Diss. Notre Dame 1960. Ann Arbor: University Microfilms, 1960.

_____ *Person in the World.* Boston: Kluwer Academic Publishers, 1997.

Batzdorff, Susanne M., Trans. *Edith Stein, Selected Writings.* Springfield: Templegate, 1996.

Beevers, John. *St. Teresa of Avila.* New York: Hanover House, 1961.

Calvert, Alexander. *The Catholic Literary Revival.* Milwaukee: Bruce Publishing Co., 1935.

Canonizzazione Della Beata Benedetta Della Croce Edith Stein. Piazza San Pietro, Ottobre 1998.

The Cambridge Companion to Aquinas. Eds. Norman Kretzmann and Eleanore Stump. Cambridge: Cambridge University Press, 1993.

Cassidy, Cardinal Edward et al. *We Remember: A Reflection on the Shoah.* Washington, DC: National Conference of Catholic Bishops, 1998.

Cohn-Sherbok, Dan. *Modern Judaism.* New York: St. Martin's Press, 1996.

DiNoia, J. Augustine, OP. *The Diversity of Religions.* Washington, DC: Catholic University Press, 1992.

Edith Stein Zum Gedanken. The Monastery. Speyer: St. Magdalena, 1987.

Eszer, Ambrose. "Edith Stein, Jewish Catholic Martyr." *Carmelite Studies* 4. Ed. John Sullivan, OCD. Washington, DC: ICS, 1987.

Eucharistiefeier und Seligsprechung von Edith Stein. Cologne, 1987.

Fisher, Eugene, "A Response to Daniel Polish." *Ecumenical Trends* (Feb. 1987), 24-27.

Flannery, Edward. *The Anguish of the Jews.* New York: Paulist Press, 1985.

The Form of Daily Prayers. Frankfurt am Main: J. Kauffmann, 1876.

Frings, Manfred C. *The Mind of Max Scheler.* Milwaukee: Marquette University, 1997.

Garber, Zev. *Shoah: The Paradigmatic Genocide.* New York: The University Press of America, 1994.

Graef, Hilda C. *The Scholar and the Cross.* Westminster, MD: Newman Press, 1955.

_____ Ed. and Trans. *Writings of Edith Stein.* London: Peter Owen Ltd., 1956.

Grieco, Gianfranco. "Un giorno di gloria nel ricordo degli orrori di distruzione e di morte." *L'Osservatore Romano* (Oct. 12-13, 1998). Author is grateful to Fr. Charles Zanoni, CS, for his courtesy in providing the English translation.

Guilead, Romaeus. *De la Phénomenologie à la Science de la Croix.* Louvain: Éditions Nauwelaertes, 1974.

Herbstrith, Waltraud, Ed. *Beten Mit Edith Stein.* Frankfurt / M: Gerhard Kaffke, 1974.

_____ *Das Wahre Gesicht Edith Steins.* Bergen-Enkheim: Gerhard Kaffke, 1971.

_____ Ed. *Edith Stein.* Mainz: Topos Taschenbücher, 1993.

_____ *Edith Stein.* Trans. Bernard Bonowitz, OCSO. San Francisco: Harper & Row, 1985. Also 2nd Ed. San Francisco: Ignatius Press, 1992.

Higgens, George G. "The Women's Challenge." *America* (Jan. 10, 1987), 3-6.

Ingarden, Roman. "Zu Edith Steins Analyse der Einfühlung und des Aufbaus der menschlichen Person" in *Denken im Dialog*. Ed. Waltraud Herbstrith. Tübingen: Attempto Verlag, 1991.

Jamart, Francois. *The Spirit and Prayer of Carmel*. Westminster, MD: Newman Press, 1951.

John Paul II, Pope. "Homily at Beatification of Edith Stein." *L'Osservatore Romano*, #20 (May 18, 1987), 19-20.

_____ "Canonization: 11 October." *L'Osservatore Romano*, #41 (Oct. 14, 1998), 1 and 10.

John XXIII, Pope. *Pacem in Terris*. Ed. William J. Gibbons, SJ. New York: Paulist Press, 1963.

Jakobovits, Immanuel, Rabbi. *Jewish Identity: Three Essays*. London: Jewish Marriage Education Council, 1971.

Kalinowski, George. "Edith Stein et Karol Wojtyla sur la personne." *Revue philosophique de Louvain*, 82 (1988), 345- 61.

Kasper, Walter. *The Christian Understanding of Freedom and the History of Freedom in the Modern Era*. Milwaukee: Marquette University Press, 1988.

Kavanaugh, Kieran, Rev. "The Canonization Process of Edith Stein," a talk given at the Washington Theological Union, Washington, DC (Nov. 7, 1997).

Keeler, Bob. "The Road to Edith Stein's Sainthood." *The Hebrew Catholic*, 64 (Nov. 1996-Feb. 1997), pp. 23, 29-30.

Kawa, Elisabeth. *Edith Stein*. Berlin: Morus Verlag, 1963.

La Farge, John, SJ. *Interracial Justice*. New York: Arno Press, 1978.

"La Phénoménologie." *Journées d'études de la Société Thomiste*. Juvisy: Les Editions du Cerf, 1932.

Lenz-Médoc, Paulus. "L'idée de l'État chez Edith Stein." *Les Études Philosophiques* (1956, #3), 456-57.

Leuven, Romaeus, OCD. *Heil im Unheil*. Freiburg: Herder, 1983.

The Liturgy of the Hours. New York: Catholic Book Publishing Co., 1975.

Maritain, Jacques. *A Christian Looks at the Jewish Question*. New York: Arno Press, 1973.

Masse, Benjamin L., SJ. *Justice for All.* Milwaukee: Bruce Publishing Co., 1964.

Matrimony — Papal Teachings. Ed. Benedictine Monks of Solesmes. Trans. Michael J. Byrnes. Boston: St. Paul Editions, 1963.

Mirabel, Elizabeth de. *Edith Stein.* Paris: Éditions du Seuil, 1954.

The New Dictionary of Theology. Ed. Joseph A. Komonchak et al. Collegeville: Liturgical Press, 1981.

Neyer, Maria Amata, Ed. *Edith Stein — Vom Endlichen zum Ewigen.* Kevelaer: Butzon & Bercker, 1973.

Oben, Freda M. "Edith Stein in Light of the Beatitudes." *Pastoral Life,* 38 #2 (1989), 28-34.

_____ "Edith Stein: Holiness in the Twentieth Century." *Spirituality Today.* Vol. 35 #2 (Summer 1983).

_____ *Edith Stein: Scholar Feminist Saint.* New York: Alba House, 1988.

Oesterreicher, John M., Msgr. *The New Encounter Between Christians and Jews.* New York: Philosophical Library, 1986.

Perspectives on We Remember: A Reflection on the Shoah. New York: The American Jewish Committee, 1998.

Polish, Daniel. "A Painful Legacy: Jews and Catholics Struggle to Understand Edith Stein and Auschwitz." *Ecumenical Trends,* 16 #9 (Oct. 1987), 153-55.

_____ "Reply to Eugene Fisher." *Ecumenical Trends* (Feb. 1988), 27-28.

_____ "The Canonization of Edith Stein." *Never Forget.* Ed. Waltraud Herbstrith, OCD. Trans. Susanne Batzdorff. Washington: ICS, 1998.

Posselt, Teresia Renata de Spiritu Sancto, OCD. *Edith Stein.* Trans. Cecily Hastings and Donald Nicholl. New York: Sheed and Ward, 1952.

Przywara, Erich. *Gebet in die Zeit.* Salzburg: O. Muller, 1946.

Quasten, Johannes, Rev. "The Waters of Refreshment." *Catholic Biblical Quarterly,* I (1939), 325-352.

Rohrbach, Peter Thomas, OCD. *Journey to Carith.* Garden City: Doubleday & Co., 1966.

Rosenzweig, Franz. *The Star of Redemption.* Trans. William W. Hallo. Boston: Beacon Press, 1972.

Scheler, Max. *Formalism in Ethics and Non-Formal Ethics of Virtue.* Trans. Manfred S. Frings et al. Evanston: Northwestern University Press, 1973.

_____ *Person and Self-Value: Three Essays.* Trans. and Ed. Manfred Frings. Boston: Kluwer Academic Publishers, 1987.

Schneider, Oda. *Im Anfang war das Herz.* Salzburg: O. Muller, 1951.

Sevretan, Philibert. "The Self and the Other in the Thought of Edith Stein." *Husserliana* 6 (1977), pp. 87-98.

Slade, Carole. *St. Teresa of Avila: author of a heroic life.* Berkeley: University of California Press, 1995.

Sokolowski, Robert. *Introduction to Phenomenology.* Cambridge: Cambridge University Press, 2000.

Spiegelberg, Herbert. *The Phenomenological Movement.* The Hague: Martinus Nyhoff, 1960.

Spieler, Josef et al. "Deutschland Bildungs-u. Erziehungswesen." *Lexikon der Pädagogik der Gegenwart.* Vol. I. Ed. Joseph Spieler. Freiburg im Breisgau: Herder, 1930.

Stein, Edith. *Aus der Tiefe Leben.* Ed. Waltraud Herbstrith. München: Kösel-Verlag, 1988.

_____ *Beiträge zur philosophischen Begründung der Psychologie und der Geisteswissenschaften.* Tübingen: Max Niemeyer, 1970.

_____ *Der Aufbau der Menschlichen Person.* Freiburg: Herder, 1994.

_____ *Endliches und Ewiges Sein.* (EES) Eds. Lucy Gelber and Romaeus Leuven, OCD, Freiburg: Herder, 1986. Author gratefully acknowledges courtesy of Ms. Augusta Spiegelman Gooch, whose unpublished translation of this text has been a source of help. The ICS plans to publish a definitive edition soon.

_____ *Essays on Woman.* Trans. Freda Mary Oben. Washington, DC: Institute of Carmelite Studies, 1987. (Essays)

_____ *The Hidden Life.* Trans. Waltraut Stein. Washington, DC: Institute of Carmelite Studies, 1992. (HL)

_____ *Husserls Phänomenologie und die Philosophie der hl. Thomas von Aquino* in *Festschrift Edmund Husserl zum 70*

Gebürtstagwidmet. Halle: Niemeyer, 1929. The English reader is directed to Sr. Catherine Baseheart's diss. on this study.

_____ *"Individuum und Gemeinschaft"* in Stein, *Beiträge.*

_____ *Knowledge and Faith.* Trans. Walter Redmond. Washington, DC: Institute of Carmelite Studies, 2000.

_____ *Life in a Jewish Family.* Trans. Josephine Koeppel, OCD. Washington, DC: Institute of Carmelite Studies, 1987.

_____ *On the Problem of Empathy.* Trans. Waltraut Stein. Washington, DC: Institute of Carmelite Studies, 1989.

_____ *"Psychische Kausalität"* in Stein, *Beiträge.*

_____ *The Science of the Cross.* Trans. Hilda Graef. Chicago: Henry Regnery Co., 1960.

_____ *Self-Portrait in Letters 1916-1942.* Trans. Josephine Koeppel, OCD. Washington, DC: Institute of Carmelite Studies, 1993. (*S-P*)

_____ *"Eine Untersuchung über den Staat"* in Stein, *Beiträge.*

Thomas Aquinas, St. *Summa Theologica.* Trans. Fathers of the English Dominican Province. New York: Benziger Bros., Inc., 1949. Vol. I.

The Woman in the Modern World. Eds. The Monks of Solesmes. Boston: Daughters of St. Paul, 1959.

ST PAULS

This book was designed and published by St. Pauls/ Alba House, the publishing arm of the Society of St. Paul, an international religious congregation of priests and brothers dedicated to serving the Church through the communications media. For information regarding this and associated ministries of the Pauline Family of Congregations, write to the Vocation Director, Society of St. Paul, 7050 Pinehurst, Dearborn, Michigan 48126. Phone (313) 582-3798 or check our internet site, www.albahouse.org